LANGUAGE OF WAR, LANGUAGE OF PEACE

RAJA SHEHADEH is Palestine's leading writer. He is also a lawyer and the founder of the pioneering Palestinian human rights organisation Al-Haq. Shehadeh is the author of several acclaimed books including *Strangers in the House* and *Occupation Diaries* and winner of the 2008 Orwell Prize for *Palestinian Walks* (all Profile). He lives in Ramallah in Palestine.

RAJA SHEHADEH

LANGUAGE OF WAR, LANGUAGE OF PEACE

Palestine, Israel and the Search for Justice

PROFILE BOOKS

First published in Great Britain in 2015 by
PROFILE BOOKS LTD
3 Holford Yard
Bevin Way
London WC1X 9HD
www.profilebooks.com

Extracts from *Cure at Troy*, by Seamus Heaney (Faber and Faber, 1990)
and from 'Burnt Norton', *Four Quartets* by T. S. Eliot (Faber and Faber,
2001) reproduced with kind permission of Faber and Faber.

1 3 5 7 9 10 8 6 4 2

Typeset in Swift by MacGuru Ltd
info@macguru.org.uk

A CIP catalogue record for this book is available from the British Library.

ISBN 978 1 78125 376 2
eISBN 978 1 78283 121 1

To my father, Aziz Shehadeh (1912–1985), who was an early advocate of peace between Palestinian Arabs and Israeli Jews and who believed that peace could bring benefits to both people

CONTENTS

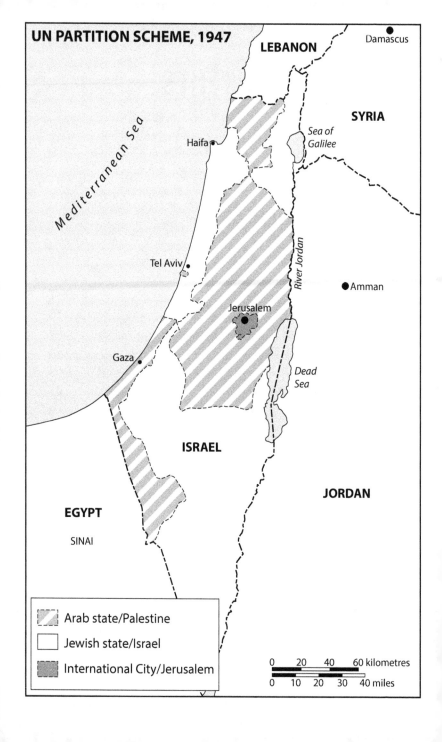

UN PARTITION SCHEME, 1947

LEBANON

Damascus

SYRIA

Mediterranean Sea

Haifa

Sea of Galilee

Tel Aviv

River Jordan

Amman

Jerusalem

Gaza

Dead Sea

ISRAEL

JORDAN

EGYPT

SINAI

Arab state/Palestine

Jewish state/Israel

International City/Jerusalem

0 20 40 60 kilometres

0 10 20 30 40 miles

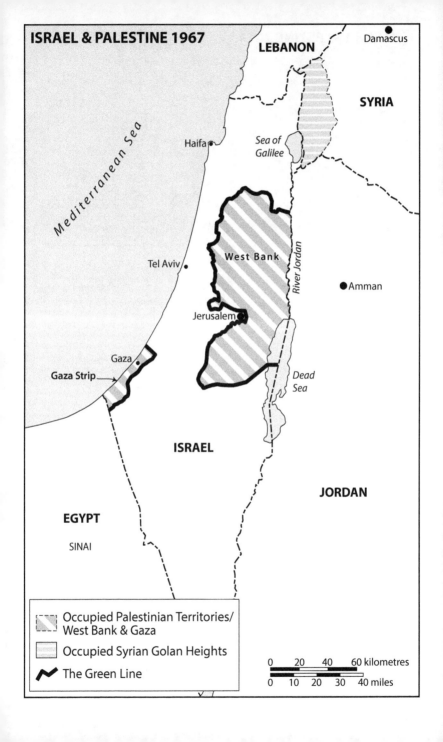

ISRAEL & PALESTINE 1967

LEBANON

Damascus

SYRIA

Mediterranean Sea

Haifa

Sea of
Galilee

West Bank

River Jordan

Tel Aviv

Amman

Jerusalem

Gaza

Gaza Strip

Dead
Sea

ISRAEL

JORDAN

EGYPT

SINAI

Occupied Palestinian Territories/
West Bank & Gaza

Occupied Syrian Golan Heights

The Green Line

| 0 | 20 | 40 | 60 kilometres |
| 0 | 10 | 20 | 30 | 40 miles |

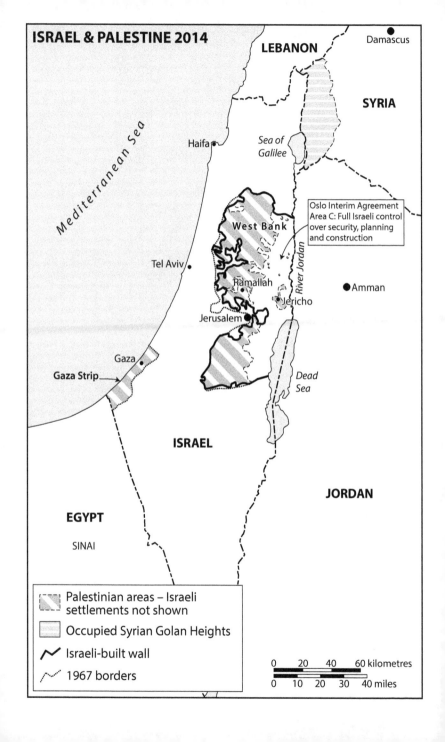

ISRAEL & PALESTINE 2014

LEBANON

Damascus

SYRIA

Mediterranean Sea

Haifa

Sea of Galilee

West Bank

Oslo Interim Agreement
Area C: Full Israeli control
over security, planning
and construction

Tel Aviv

Ramallah

River Jordan

Amman

Jericho

Jerusalem

Gaza

Dead Sea

Gaza Strip

ISRAEL

JORDAN

EGYPT

SINAI

Palestinian areas – Israeli
settlements not shown

Occupied Syrian Golan Heights

Israeli-built wall

1967 borders

0   20   40   60 kilometres

0   10   20   30   40 miles

1

1948: INFILTRATING BACK HOME

'I asked myself: "Does a drowning man take up fishing?"'
Emile Habibi, *Saraya bint al-Ghul*

This book is based on the Edward Said memorial lectures I gave at Columbia University, New York, on 17 October 2013 and the British Museum, London, on 28 March 2014 to mark the ten years since Edward's death. His penetrating intelligence, humanism and commitment to the Palestinian cause continue to be sorely missed. As events unfold in our troubled region, I often wonder how he would respond. In this book I have tried to be guided by Edward, reflecting on the issues that were the focus of his interest: culture, language and politics. And as I am a lawyer the legal issues are also of particular interest to me, so I comment on these as well.

When I gave these two lectures, the US-sponsored peace negotiations were still in progress. Few believed that they would come to anything, but my own persistent optimism led me to hope. I longed to be able to end the book with a description of the terms of the negotiated settlement that had moved this long-standing conflict closer to a just resolution. But it was not to be. My original title, 'Language of Peace', has sadly had to be modified with the addition of 'Language of War'. And yet still I have been guided by Edward's often-repeated aphorism, borrowed from Antonio Gramsci: 'Pessimism of the intellect, optimism of the will.'

Readers will find plenty to induce pessimism in the developments that I describe here. Over the years matters have gone in only one direction, from bad to worse, and anyone with a critical intellect will surely reflect on the present condition of the Palestinians with despair. But we cannot allow intellect to be the only measure. I have always believed, and have not given up hope, that a new generation of Israelis and Palestinians will one day look around and realise that they can no longer accept the way their elders have organised their lives. Indeed, they are not truly living a life, whether they are in the camp of the oppressed or the oppressors. Divine intervention is not going to save either of us; we have to save ourselves. I am convinced that, however long it takes, the optimism of the will is ultimately bound to triumph.

In saying this, I am in no way denying the painful past, and fully recognise the tremendous suffering and injustice

2

the present order has subjected the Palestinians to, as this book will make clear.

The future of this small area between the Mediterranean Sea and the River Jordan is the concern of not only Israelis and Palestinians. It is a land with particular significance to many people around the world. It has been known for a long time that the key to a safer, more peaceful Middle East lies in resolving the conflict here. While it will ultimately fall upon those of us who live in this tiny contested plot to make peace possible, at the moment we cannot achieve this without the assistance of the rest of the world.

I came to terms long ago with the fact that books have limited power to affect history and politics. Yet my optimism keeps me hopeful that by helping readers to better understand what is taking place here and by proposing things they can do to make change possible, the cause of peace will be furthered. In this way I have tried to remain truthful to Edward Said's unshakeable belief in the ultimate optimism of the will, while doing my best to present an honest and critical assessment of the current situation.

❧

One evening in the summer of 2013 – just after receiving the invitation to give the first lecture – I was at the grandly named Cultural Palace in Ramallah, watching a play called *Sagh Salim* (Healthy and Whole). This one-man autobiographical piece by Salim Dao, a Palestinian resident of Haifa, started me thinking about the status of Palestinians in historic Palestine and how the language used to describe them has changed over time: from 'citizens' in Mandate

Palestine to 'infiltrators' and 'absentees' under Israeli law and then to 'meddlers' and 'terrorists'.

On the stage, Dao – short, thin, shaven-headed, bespectacled – was sitting on a suitcase, his expression intense and sorrowful. He began the play by begging the audience for their understanding, then announced that, after much thought, he had decided to leave the country. However, before departing he wanted to talk: 'I have so much to say, years of words,' he declared. But he warned us that once he started talking he would be unable to stop shaking: 'This is not a play. You have come to see someone who doesn't know what to do with himself. Let me first begin by telling you where I come from. I was born and grew up in the Galilean village of El Baaneh.'

With satire and self-deprecating humour, he proceeded to tell his life story, from the time he was born – a few years after the Nakba (catastrophe) of 1948 – to the present. He mused on how as a child he could not understand why neighbours from the village who had managed to return home after their expulsion in the months of active war during 1948 were described as *mutasalilun* (infiltrators). As he spoke the word, his face assumed an expression of perplexity, sadness, resilience and weary endurance. He was almost in tears as he asked, 'These were neighbours, their homes in the village, so how did they become outlaws who could only be mentioned in whispers?'

The forlorn yet obdurate expression on Salim's face as he hesitantly, almost guiltily, uttered the word 'infiltrators' was one that I immediately recognised as quintessentially Palestinian. It continued to haunt me after the performance and I was still thinking of it a few days later as I drove down to the Jordan Valley through the lunar hills between Jerusalem and Jericho. I passed many signposts for recently built Jewish settlements served by roads that we Palestinians cannot use. How odd, having separate roads for different ethnic groups, as well as different categories of land where different rules apply, and yet as I drove along I was fully aware of where I could and could not go, automatically taking the circuitous routes that confound the geography of the region.

It was Salim Dao's play that alerted me to what I was doing. As I drove, I wondered how many more terms and behaviours I have unwittingly adopted, and to what extent I have made the language of occupation and defeat my own.

I've become accustomed to so much. I have almost forgotten that I used to take the pleasant narrow road that runs through the soft hills leading to the attractive village of Beitin, north of Ramallah. I have not visited Beitin for over fifteen years, but I remember that landmark house near the pine tree that one saw on first entering the village. This road is now reserved solely for privileged VIPs with cards issued by Israel, as well as foreign dignitaries visiting Palestinian officials in Ramallah. We have stopped calling it the Beitin road and now refer to it as the DCO (District Coordination Office) road. Just as I've become used to the new network of roads, so I've become used to the language of occupation and oppression that determines our small world ... to the extent that I have stopped thinking about it.

This led me to reflect further on the linguistic oddities we have had to train ourselves to accept in order to get on with our daily lives in the Israeli-occupied territories, sometimes called the State of Palestine. In what follows I

will explore how these terms have entered our consciousness and become so much a part of our lives that we no
longer notice them. I will then go on to discuss what I call
the legal narratives of the two protagonists, Israel and
Palestine, and consider how and why the Israeli narrative
has prevailed. I will briefly review the troubled nine-month
course of the latest US-sponsored peace talks, which have
come to nothing, and see what lessons we can draw from
this failure. Finally, I will show how the language of peace
turned into the language of war, and consider what it will
now take to arrive at peace in our troubled region.

Only a few of the Palestinians forced out of their homes by
Israel in 1947–8 were bold enough to try to return immediately. Some were shot at and died, but others survived
and tried again. Some of them made it and managed to get
the much-coveted identity card that the new government
issued after the establishment of the State of Israel, but
they then lived the rest of their lives in fear that the Israeli
authorities would find out that they were so-called 'infiltrators' and deport them.

However, most displaced Palestinians decided to wait
until the hostilities ended before trying to return to their
homes. They were given tents and provisions to help them
survive by the Red Cross. That winter of 1948–9 was one of
the coldest the region had ever known. How odd it is that
every time people here are forced out, nature conspires to
produce a harsh winter: this was again the case in 2013,
when Syrian refugees in Jordan endured one of the worst
winters on record.

Anyway, here is our first twist in terminology. The Palestinians who were forced out of their homes in 1948 were not regarded by Israel as refugees. That would have implied that Palestine was their country, to which they should be allowed to return. This was not how the Israeli authorities saw it, on either count, and they did their best to make sure that the return would never happen. The Palestinians who were forced out of their homes and country, whom Israel called 'infiltrators' when they tried to return, were not defined by the UN as refugees, with the full rights accorded to this category of people the world over. Not only did Israel ban Palestinian refugees from returning home, as it continues to do to this day, but in denying them refugee status it also denied their existence as a national group. Rather than being placed under the auspices of the United Nations High Commissioner for Refugees (UNHCR) and being subject to the legal regime of international refugees (as established in 1951), they were accorded 'special status' and a specific unit was created by the UN to take care of them. This was the United Nations Relief and Works Agency for Palestinian Refugees in the Near East, from whose usual acronym, UNRWA, the mention of 'refugees' is remarkably absent.[1]

The significance of this distinction remains of great importance to this day. In reporting on a survey published on 19 June 2013 by UNHCR, the *Guardian* noted that by the end of 2012 the number of forcibly displaced people worldwide had reached 45.2 million, including 15.4 million refugees. This prompted a reader to write to the editor:

> you completely failed to quote the number of Palestinian refugees, citing instead that the largest number

of refugees, by country of origin, is from Afghanistan, at 2,585,600. What you omitted, presumably by choice, is the information from the same UN report that the article is based on, as follows: 'of 10.5 million refugees under UNHCR's mandate ... a further 4.9 million Palestinian refugees fall under the mandate of its sister agency, the UN Relief and Works Agency' ... I am curious as to why your article completely omits to mention the Palestinian refugees. Surely, as the largest group of refugees in the world, they should merit some mention?

Chris Elliott, the readers' editor, responded in the Open Door section of the paper on 28 July 2013:

The heart of the problem – which we should have realised sooner – lies in the fact that the Palestinian refugees do indeed fall under the mandate of the United Nations Relief and Works Agency (UNRWA) not UNHCR. According to the UNRWA website this is because: 'As UNRWA was set up in 1949, Palestine refugees were specifically and intentionally excluded from the international refugee law regime established in 1951. The 1951 Convention relating to the Status of Refugees and the 1967 Protocol thereto exclude Palestine refugees as long as they receive assistance from UNRWA. The UN office of the High Commissioner for Refugees (UNHCR) provides assistance and protection to Palestine refugees outside UNRWA's areas of operations.' ... that's why Afghanistan tops the chart [of UNHCR statistics] ... The only Palestinian refugees who do appear in the UNHCR statistics are 94,804 who are in countries where UNRWA doesn't operate, and thus fall under the protection of the refugee agency.

So began our long ordeal of confinement by exclusivist categorisation. Palestinian refugees became a special category, different from refugees the world over, and, as we shall see, they were considered 'absentees', a category without context which meant they were denied compensation and the right of return. But who were these absentee owners? Had they somehow just absented themselves from homes and property that belonged to them?

An Israeli law of 1950 defined an 'absentee' as someone who, between 29 November 1947 and the date when the state of emergency ceased to exist, happened to be outside Palestine, regardless of the reason – they could have been abroad for business, study or their health. As such, they lost their right to return home and were denied access to their property.[2] It should be noted that the law considers the start date as 29 November 1947, the date of United Nations Resolution 181 on the partition of Palestine, which recommended the creation of an Arab and Jewish state in Palestine, and not when the much larger State of Israel was declared.

The line these refugees were hoping to cross in their attempt to return home following Israel's creation came to be called the Green Line – purely because of the colour of the ink used on the map demarcating the 1949 Armistice Agreements between Israel and Jordan. Desperate to deter more Israeli settlers from crossing the line that had served as the border for nineteen years, between 1948 to 1967, the

Palestinian Authority (PA)[3] tried in March 2014 to have the UN change the colour of this demarcation line from green to red, arguing that the arbitrary line representing Israel's pre-1967 borders was sending out the wrong message. In explaining why they were calling for this change, one Palestinian official explained, 'What does green say to you? Green means go, right? But what about the colour red? Red says stop. For all these years those settlers have been pouring over the Green Line. Now we want the UN to deliver a clear message to Israelis: stop when you see red.'[4]

Meanwhile, the Arab Jews who were being absorbed into Israel after 1948 were not called refugees either. They arrived through *ma'abarot* (transit), as though by coming to Israel they were en route to heaven. In Hebrew they were said to have made *aliya* (ascent). They were not mere immigrants to the new country. Instead, according to the Zionist ethos, they were returnees who had come home after 2,000 years of exile. On 25 September 2013 the Israeli High Court rejected the appeal of twenty-one appellants who wanted their nationality to be listed as 'Israeli' rather than 'Jewish' in the Population Registry. Palestinians, who are often accused of denying the existence of Israel, on occasion find a strange ally in the High Court.

Advocating a binational solution, Edward Said wrote in 1999: 'The beginning is to develop something entirely missing from both Israeli and Palestinian realities today: the idea and practice of citizenship, not of ethnic or racial community, as the main vehicle of coexistence.'[5] How far we are from reaching this ideal.

From its earliest days the Zionist movement was focused not only on winning the military struggle but also on how to interpret history and classify those who were the original inhabitants of the land, both Palestinian Arabs and Jews. This is something Edward often remarked upon and tried so energetically to expose through his writings on Palestine. That Palestinian refugees became a special category different from other refugees and absentees became a category without context, thus denied compensation and the right of return, are fundamental to our problem. To this day Israel refuses to have an immigration law like other countries.

Putting aside Israel's refusal to allow back any Palestinian refugee, its record of accepting non-Jewish refugees and asylum seekers is one of the worst in the world, even though it is a signatory to the 1951 Convention Relating to the Status of Refugees. Out of a total of 17,194 applications, only twenty-six were approved between July 2009 and August 2013.[6]

In its attempts to rewrite history, Israel is unintentionally supported by the bureaucracies of international organisations. Until recently UNRWA, for example, made access to its archives very difficult. The International Committee of the Red Cross (ICRC) has at its archive in Geneva a collection of photographs of Palestine/Israel taken between 1947 and 1950. These are accessible to the public but, according to Ariella Azoulay in her 2012 study *Different Ways Not to Say Deportation. Unshowable Photographs: An Introduction*:

> In order to show them, one needs the permission of the ICRC. Permission depends on the ICRC's approval of any text that an archive user might write to accompany the photographs ... By controlling the way photographs

are described in public, the archive sentries appear authorized to deny citizens the right to freely read their history, show it to others, reinterpret it, share it, and imagine another future out of it.[7]

And the category distinctions continued. There were also 'internal absentees' or, as they are sometimes referred to, 'present absentees', as well as 'internal infiltrators'. These are Palestinians who never left Palestine; they just temporarily moved away from their village to stay in another part of Palestine that then became Israel, but when they tried to go back they were prevented. This prohibition against returning to their original village continues to this day. All they could do was steal on to their land to collect edible or medicinal wild herbs, risking arrest by the authorities. An Israeli organisation called Zochrot (Remembering), which was founded in 2002, held an international conference in the first week of October 2013 at the Eretz Israel Museum to discuss ways of promoting the return of Palestinian refugees. Amir Mashkar, a participant, spoke about the outpost which he and his friends had set up at the church in Ikrit, one of the Palestinian villages whose inhabitants were forced out in 1948 and were not allowed to return after the war, although they had remained in Israel. He told the conference, 'There was no longer a war, the war was over, there weren't any confrontations, and suddenly the village disappeared. Only the church and cemetery remained ... to this day we bury our dead in Ikrit. We return to our village only as corpses.'[8]

Among the internal absentees was the poet Taha Muhammad Ali, from the village of Saffuriyya in the

Galilee, who did not leave Palestine yet still could not return to his village. He settled in nearby Nazareth and in spring and summer he and his fellow villagers would steal on to their land to surreptitiously gather the wild herbs growing there, inspiring his 1983 poem 'Ambergris':[9]

This land denies,
Cheats and betrays us;
We're too much for it;
It grumbles about us –
Detests us.
Its newcomers,
Sailors and usurpers,
Uproot the backyard gardens,
Burying the trees.
They keep us from looking too long
At the anemone blossom and cyclamen,
And won't allow us to touch the herbs,
And wild artichoke and chicory.

❧

Granting Palestinians in Israel citizenship was a shrewd act on the part of the new Israeli authorities. In many ways it was a sleight of hand to show the new state in a good light. What Israeli leaders were really working on were ways to both withstand international pressure to allow Palestinian refugees re-entry and encourage those who had stayed to leave. In June 1950, Moshe Dayan, then head of the Southern Command of the Israeli Army, said, 'The 170,000 Arabs who remain in the country should be treated as though their fate has not yet been sealed. I hope that, in the years ahead, another possibility might arise to implement a transfer of those Arabs from the Land of Israel.' A transfer committee was established under the chairmanship of Yosef Weitz of the Jewish National Fund, one of whose recommendations was that the Arabs' abandonment of their homes should be considered an irrevocable fait accompli and that Israel should support their resettlement elsewhere. The committee also recommended that Arabs who had remained in the country should be encouraged to emigrate and that the state should buy the land of Arabs who were willing to leave. In addition, Arab villages should be destroyed and Arabs should be prevented from working the land, harvesting field crops and picking olives.[10]

But these were secret deliberations. Israel's Declaration of Independence set out to show the world that Israel was a democratic state, asserting that it '... will ensure complete equality of social and political rights to all its inhabitants irrespective of religion, race or sex; it will guarantee freedom of religion, conscience, language, education and culture; it will safeguard the Holy Places of all religions; and it will be faithful to the principles of the Charter of the United Nations'.

And yet already by 1948 there were three groups of Palestinians: those who were now Israeli citizens; those who were living in or had found refuge in the West Bank, who were made Jordanian citizens; and those who were utterly stateless UNRWA refugees in the Gaza Strip, in various Arab countries and in the rest of the world. More fragmentation and differentiation were yet to come.

Over a quarter of the residents of the Gaza Strip have

relatives in the West Bank and about 15 per cent have relatives in East Jerusalem or in Israel. Even so, 'Israel's movement-restriction policy stipulates that family visits involving the entry to or exit from the Gaza Strip are only allowed to first-degree relatives and only under extraordinary circumstances such as a wedding, a death or a grave illness. These are also subject to a complex procedure of permit requests.'[11] On 21 April 2013, for example, twenty-six Gaza runners were not allowed to cross to the West Bank to take part in the Bethlehem marathon.

And yet sometimes the Palestinians of 1948 and those like me of 1967 come together. When Israel's Minister of the Economy and leader of its Habayit Hayehudi (Jewish Home) party, Naftali Bennett, was speaking about us in and to his world of Greater Israel, he compared us to shrapnel in Israel's 'butt'.[12]

Returning to the play *Sagh Salim*, we learned from Salim Dao that he and his fellow villagers knew that once you became a citizen of the new state you had to celebrate its Independence Day, otherwise you'd be viewed with suspicion. Like all other Palestinians in Israel, they were taught in school the same myth that whole generations of Israeli youth have been brought up on – namely that Israeli Jews fought and won their independence from the British. Not only does this deny the presence of the Palestinian Arabs from whom the land had to be wrenched, it also falsifies history by failing to credit the British contribution to the creation of Israel – notably the Balfour Declaration of 1917[13] and the very terms of the British Mandate in Palestine. Moreover, it places Israel rather strangely in the family of nations who have overcome imperialism and secured their independence from the coloniser. What was young Salim to make of this, when his fellow villagers were not allowed to return to their homes and were called 'infiltrators' when they tried? And how strange it must have been for those who had just lost everything to have to swallow their pride and celebrate the Independence Day of the country that had caused their Nakba.

But Salim Dao offered us a different take. In satirical mode he informed us, his Ramallah audience, that the only time he and his fellow villagers felt free was on Israel's Independence Day.

The women packed bundles of food and everyone crowded into trucks – no traffic tickets issued that day – and headed out for a picnic, cheering and singing, most loudly when they got near a police car. They reached Lake Tiberias early, spread their rugs close to the water and started their barbecue fires, singing and dancing all the while. Every year a few people died swimming. Why not? We Arabs drown in their independence.

Then in the evening we would feel sad and depressed at having to return home. Here our freedom ends ... *so that the freedom of others, which is democracy, can begin.*

This last phrase Dao declaimed loudly, as one chanting a slogan.

The regularity with which at least one Palestinian died during that excursion, drowning in the lake, reminded me of how Palestinians still perish when Israel grants the infrequent permits for residents of the West Bank to visit the sea, from which we are excluded for the rest of the year. Lacking experience of swimming in the sea, in their enthusiasm young Palestinians take unwarranted risks and almost invariably one or more drown in the euphoria of celebrating freedom for the day.

While Salim and the other estimated 16,000 Palestinians who managed to stay in what became Israel had to endure their strange new fate of not being allowed to return to their villages, the generation of Palestinians born in the West Bank after 1948 lived under Jordanian rule in almost total ignorance of what was happening in nearby Israel.

2

1967: SETTLING THE OCCUPIED TERRITORIES

'Appeals to the past are among the commonest of strategies in interpretations of the present.'

Edward Said, *Culture and Imperialism*

My father refused to register us with UNRWA after my family was forced out of our home in Jaffa and became refugees in Ramallah. Like other Palestinians who were living in the West Bank or found refuge there, we became citizens of Jordan. Our new country did its best to make us forget that we were Palestinian. Palestine was no more. Yet hardly had two decades passed when Israel went to war and in June 1967 captured the West Bank, which it has held ever since. This was hubris, the bane of all those who hold power.

Until then, those of us exiled in the West Bank had had a respite of sorts: nineteen years to work things out and get over the trauma of 1948. But in 1967 we faced another setback as our territory was fragmented again. East Jerusalem, six square kilometres in area, was annexed to Israel, along with another sixty-four square kilometres of land, most of which belonged to twenty-eight West Bank villages and the rest to the municipalities of Bethlehem and Beit Jala. This enlarged area came to be defined as Greater Jerusalem. The remainder of the occupied territories, including the Gaza Strip, was placed under Israeli military rule.

For Israel those nineteen years from 1948 to 1967 were a period of preparation for what came next. Immediately after it was established in 1948, the country created a military government to rule over the Palestinians who were granted Israeli citizenship. This military government was dissolved only six months before the next one began in the newly occupied territories of the West Bank and Gaza Strip. This meant that the Israeli governors of Arab areas under military government in Israel, mainly in the Galilee, had a six-month vacation before being moved in June 1967 to the West Bank and Gaza Strip to again establish military rule there.

Until 1967 we lived with a simple tale. From my family I heard about the heavenly Jaffa they were forced to leave. From the school curriculum we learned the geography of a historic Palestine that took no account of Israel's presence or of what the new rulers were doing to the land.

My geography teacher, Abu el-Awad, who wore the *umbaz* (traditional Arab dress), would draw the map of Palestine on the blackboard. There was the Dead Sea in the south, further north Lake Tiberias and above it another small lake, Lake Huleh. We had to memorise all this, unaware that the lake was no longer there, having been drained by the Israelis in the early 1950s (and not, incidentally – as is often claimed – because they wanted to eliminate malarial mosquitoes). We also sang (as we do to this day) of *labban el-jamouseh*, the milk of the water buffaloes that were once common there but are now extinct, just like the lake itself and the way of life of the marsh Arabs who had long flourished there. Today, Israel has created a mini Huleh as a national park, with a few imported water buffaloes forlornly scattered throughout the marshes.

We have a family photo, a rare portrait from 1968. It was taken because we were told that to obtain an Israeli laissez-passer to enable us to travel, we needed to submit a family portrait. This was false information, but the portrait stands as a reminder of those terrible first months, before we became used to the indignity and insult of living under occupation. The photo tells it all, how miserable we were after Israel occupied our town and we began to be entangled in its Kafkaesque rules. We all look distraught.

With the 1967 occupation, we in the West Bank gradually became better educated about Israeli ways. We would have had a head start had we been willing to listen to fellow Palestinians who had been through it all before, who had remained in Palestine and become Israeli citizens. None of the tactics Israel used to control us were new. The same old practices and even the same personnel, who were in charge in the first round to control those Palestinians who remained, resurfaced. Shortly after the occupation,

I remember one relative from Haifa who had become an Israeli citizen telling my father how it was going to be and what we should expect. He began by assuring us that we were still in the honeymoon period. But, he said, 'It will only be a short honeymoon. Afterwards the hardship will begin. First they will impose heavy taxes, then land acquisition will start, then what is left of the land will be rendered out of reach through land-use planning.' This was exactly what would happen. But we were not prepared to listen and take precautions. We considered those who had stayed to be the lackeys of the enemy, the defeated sector who were lorded over by their Israeli masters. Who wants to listen to the vanquished? Sadly, we failed to recognise that they were heroes who had withstood and survived, all on their own, the misery, confusion and enormous systematic pressure from Israel's exclusivist policies. But neither they nor we were glamorous – all the kudos went to those who took up arms and fought like men, not to those who practised *sumoud*, an Arabic word meaning steadfastness, endurance and perseverance in the face of adversity – all passive traits lacking in glamour.

I remember a cartoon which one acquaintance had pinned to his door showing someone being kicked on the backside. Underneath he had written the word '*sumoud*'. That we in turn would not be listened to I learned later when, in 1991, I joined the negotiations in Washington, DC, between Israel and the PLO.

The property of those who left the West Bank (including East Jerusalem) and the Gaza Strip during the war, or who happened to be away when the war took place and were prevented from getting back, was again seized by Israel.

Only this time it was not called 'absentee property' but 'abandoned property'. It no longer mattered whether or not the owners had left the area for countries which were at war with Israel. 'Abandoners' were now defined as those who were outside the area when the war ended, regardless of whether they were in warring or friendly states. It was a slight but important change. In recent years it has become clear that in the Jordan Valley alone the World Zionist Organization allocated to Jewish settlers over a thousand acres of fertile Palestinian land, including property belonging to those denied return to the occupied territories in 1967.

After the 1967 war Israel propagated the fiction that its occupation of Palestinian lands was the most benevolent in history. Yet still the ungrateful Palestinians did not take it lying down. We called those who resisted the occupation *fedayeen* (freedom fighters). Israel's word for them was *mukharebeen* (Arabic for those who destroy or ruin). Initially I wondered about this word. It is what you use when talking to a naughty child in Arabic: '*Anta mukhareb!*', 'You are a vandal!' And what, I asked myself, were we vandalising? Then I realised that Israel felt it was putting things in order for us as well as for themselves, and we were spoiling it. That was it.

❧

It took some time before we were upgraded but eventually, when US president George Bush declared his 'war on terror', we graduated to being *irhabiyeen* (terrorists). Each and every one of us, without exception: in Israel's eyes we are all potential terrorists. In fact, we Palestinians are only there by permission of the Israeli state. Those who carry a Palestinian passport are no different. The number on that passport remains the one assigned to us by Israel and recorded in their security files and databases. Israel can, on a whim, prohibit anyone from returning home by revoking their residency. This is the condition of all Palestinians now living in the Palestinian territories and East Jerusalem. An Israeli military order issued in 2009 modified the definition of 'infiltrator' given in an earlier (1969) order so as to encompass anyone who enters the West Bank illegally as well as anyone 'who is present in the Area and does not lawfully hold a permit'. The military order does not clarify what kind of permit is required and thus leaves it open for the Israeli authorities in the occupied territory to interpret as they will. According to Amnesty International, those considered to be 'infiltrators' can be deported to other states, forcibly transferred to the Gaza Strip or made to face criminal charges. This could include Palestinians whose address is recorded as being the Gaza Strip, even if they were living in or were born in the West Bank. This order was first used on 21 April 2010, when Israeli authorities deported a Palestinian prisoner to the Gaza Strip after he was released following a nine-year prison sentence. In Israel's eyes, we are all infiltrators living where we are not supposed to live.

That this has gone beyond military orders and guides the thinking and actions of soldiers on the ground was evident in the case of fourteen-year-old Yusef al-Shawamreh from the village of Deir Al Asal on the West Bank, who in the spring of 2014 went to his land to pick *akub* (gundelia), a prickly plant delicious when cooked. Yusef was shot and killed by an Israeli army captain. Asked about the incident by an Israeli from the Arab-Israeli organisation Ta'ayush who came to investigate it, the unrepentant captain replied, 'This is mine, I am the law here, I am the sovereign.'[1]

Ihab Ahmad Sawalha, a young man from Asira ash-Shamaliya, a village north of Nablus, was not shot dead but is suffering the consequences of being called a terrorist. When he was born, an official at the Rafidya Hospital in Nablus made a clerical error, adding a superfluous 'r' and registering his name as Irhab (terrorism) rather than Ihab. And so it remained on the Palestinian Authority Identity Card that was issued to him when he turned sixteen. With such a name Ihab's life is hell. When Israeli soldiers see his name at checkpoints, they refuse to allow him to pass. He had to leave school because he was cruelly teased by his classmates. And now that he is of working age he cannot get a permit to work in Israel. You might think Ihab's problem could be easily solved by requesting a correction of his name on the ID card. But even though the Palestinian Authority issues these cards, authorisation has to come from Israel, which still controls the population register, for the initial issuing and for every change made subsequently. Thus far the Israeli authorities have refused to correct Ihab's name, so he has to endure life in the occupied territories being called Terrorism.

All these designations, categorisations and prohibitions are intended primarily to keep us on edge, to make us culpable for merely living on our land. The numerous checkpoints that make our lives so difficult and which fragment our territory serve no security purpose, as events in the summer of 2013 illustrated.

Two days into Eid al-Fitr in July 2013, Israel decided to lift the barriers at crossing points leading from the West Bank to East Jerusalem and the rest of Israel. Immediately, huge crowds gathered to make the most of this opportunity, going on to Jerusalem, Jaffa and the Galilee. Some saw the sea for the first time. As usual, one young man, this time from Nablus, drowned off the shore of Jaffa. There was no need for permits, no stamping of documents or any checks, making it possible for even those with a security record to go through. So much for the security argument that, according to Israel, makes these checkpoints necessary. In their kindness, for two days the Israeli authorities allowed Palestinians to enjoy the land they dream of, before the gates were shut again.

For about a year and a half Gil Hilel, from the group Breaking the Silence, served as an Israeli soldier in Hebron. This is how she described her experience:

> I lived the reality of Occupation. Like other male and female soldiers serving in the Occupied Territories, I learned soon enough the kind of conduct acceptable and expected of me as a combatant in this reality. I learned to do the job assigned to me – controlling Palestinians. I learned to speak the language of occupation, a language of imperatives and demands. It became my mother-tongue.
>
> In the reality of occupation there are no Palestinian civilians, there are only potential terrorists. Any Palestinian man might attack any moment, any Palestinian

woman is dangerous. They have no face and no rights. Our job is to rule. To do that, we must make the Palestinians obey us, and they will only obey if they are afraid of us.[2]

Simon Jenkins gave one of the best definitions of terrorism in an article published in the *Guardian*: 'Terrorism is a specific and rational political form: the use of violence to achieve a multiplier of fear through a civilian population to a particular end.'[3] Applying this definition, the actions of the Jewish settlers who carry out so-called 'price tag' hate crimes – random acts of violence aimed at the Palestinian population and Israeli security forces, including assaults, defacing and vandalising tombstones, burning mosques and churches, and destroying cars in Jerusalem's Arab neighbourhoods – whether in the West Bank or Jerusalem, would constitute terrorism. But Israel does not see it that way. For Israel the determining factor is religion. Whereas a Palestinian can be a terrorist, an Israeli Jew who performs actions that amount to terrorism in both their nature and their objective would, except in rare cases, be merely defined as belonging to an 'illegal organisation'. For Israeli citizens, whether or not an action is defined as terrorism has material consequences: victims of terrorism receive compensation from the state. In Israel this derogatory designation is rarely ascribed to Jews. Eden Natan Zada, who murdered four Arab citizens of Israel in a shooting spree in Shfaram in August 2005 before he was killed, was not defined as a terrorist. In justification of their decision, the Israeli State Prosecutor's Office declared that they did not want to 'defame the dead'.

❧

For over three decades now I have been writing about the human rights aspects of the occupation and the illegality of the Jewish settlements. My first book on the legal aspects of the occupation was published in 1980, two years after I returned from my law studies in London. Since then I have been trying to figure out what is going on in my country and how the most intricate and abstruse legal language is being employed to claim that the attrition is taking place in a perfectly legal manner.

In my 1982 book *The Third Way*, I wrote about a drive I took in the winter of that year with a cousin visiting from Amman:

Today I took my cousin ... to Jericho, which is the best place to go in the winter ... As we rode down I was thinking to myself how blessed we have been with the rains this year ... The thought was killed by my cousin, who read out in scathing tones the road sign that has been set up at the entrance to Jericho, in English and Hebrew – not in Arabic: Welcome to Tamar Regional Council.

'Is that where we're going? I had supposed in my innocence that we were driving to Ariha [the Arab name for Jericho]. I bet next thing you know, you will wake up to find that you too have been allotted a Hebrew name with 2,000-year-old credentials,' my cousin said.

I was silent. Ahead of us, we saw several parked station wagons. A few bearded men in black, heavy overcoats, sweating profusely in the heat of the day, were digging holes for poles and taking measurements.

Scurrying back and forth was an American-looking blond man, his big belly bulging over his trousers.

'So, a new Jewish settlement's in the making!' sneered my cousin. 'Why don't you do anything about them – don't you have any pride?'

Thirty-two years have passed since then, many of them spent writing to bring to the world's attention the dangers of these colonial activities, but to no avail. In the same book I describe a strange visit I received at my law office from two Israeli Jews from Ofra, a settlement situated north of Ramallah, established almost exclusively on privately owned Palestinian lands. The settlers asked me to register a company for them. When I refused, Aharon, their spokesman, responded:

'Why not? We live in Ofra, you live in Ramallah. We have expertise we can offer you, just as you have expertise to offer us. Why should any of the locals refuse to do business with us? We are bringing progress to the area. Do you want to say you're against that?'

... I made it clear to him that 'most Palestinians feel as I do and they will not want to have anything to do with the settlers.'

'But why? We are not depriving you of anything. The more settlements the more progress. How can that be bad for you?' he answered.

Aharon could not or did not want to understand. He has been at it ever since.

3

1993: OSLO ACCORDS
– A POST-MORTEM

'The annulment of all measures of annexation and appropriation and the removal of settlements established by Israel in the Palestinian and Arab territories since 1967.'

Communiqué outlining the objective of the Palestinian
National Council, meeting in Algiers, 15 November 1988

Over time the number of Jewish settlers increased and by far the lion's share of the scarce resources of the West Bank were exploited by them. Israel was hoping we Palestinians would get exhausted and leave. But this did not happen. In the myopia of its triumph Israel fails to realise how adaptable human beings are and how resourceful and resilient Palestinians have learned to be. When they close one road, we find another; we are like water that invariably finds new channels in a stream. *Sumoud* is a rocky road – often derided, sometimes set aside – but it is the surest way to survive. If we learned anything from the Nakba it was that whatever happens we will never again leave our homes. During the 2002 invasion my octogenarian mother, still regretting leaving Jaffa as a young mother, insisted on staying in her house in the centre of Ramallah, even when five Israeli tanks were parked close by and firing at nearby buildings.

By 1987 the number of *mukharebeen* became plentiful in the occupied territories. Practically all of us became saboteurs and spoilers. We used every non-violent means – boycott, civil resistance – and some violent ones to show that we'd had enough of occupation and would not stop our civil resistance until it ended. The first Intifada had begun. The military struggle, such as it was, had brought no results. The non-violent first Intifada waged inside the occupied territories finally brought Israel to the negotiating table. Five years later, Israel was persuaded to attend the international peace conference in Madrid from 30 October to 1 November 1991, and eventually began negotiating with the Palestinian delegation, which was then formally called the joint Jordanian-Palestinian delegation.[1] But the external Palestinian leadership in Tunis hardly recognised the important role that those of us living under Israeli rule were playing in the struggle. This I was to discover when acting as legal adviser to the bilateral negotiations that began in Washington, DC, in December 1991. I remember Edward Said coming to Washington expressly to offer his services to the delegation, only to be refused. With the

30

extensive media interest at the time, he could have played a crucial role, explaining to the American public what was taking place at the negotiations. What sort of leadership refuses an offer of help from a giant like Said?

It was clear to me that Israel's strategy in the negotiations was to try its best to retain the almost one thousand military orders, amending local law and adding to it, that governed every aspect of life in the occupied territories and organised relations between Palestinian Arabs and Israeli Jews there. Different orders applied to the two groups living in the same area, discriminating between them in terms of allocation of land, use of the natural resources and possibilities for development and growth. Using the vehicle of military orders, Israeli laws were imported but applied exclusively to the settlers. Had the settlements been made to submit to the same restrictive and oppressive military orders to which Israel was subjecting the Palestinians, it would not have been possible for them to survive, let alone prosper and expand. There had to be apartheid (separate and unequal development) if Jewish settlements were to flourish.

In 1991–2, throughout my time at the bilateral negotiations that took place with Israel and the joint Jordanian-Palestinian delegation in Washington and that preceded direct negotiations in Oslo, one question kept nagging at me: how had Israel succeeded in using more or less the same tactics against Palestinians and their property in 1967 that they had used in 1948? Why had we Palestinians not learned how to foil these tactics?

After a year of desperately trying to impress upon the leadership the need for a legal strategy based on a review of the military orders that underpinned the apartheid – like discrimination between Palestinians and Jewish residents of the occupied territories – instructions arrived from Tunis on 13 September 1992 that a review of the military orders would be harmful, since this would only give the orders recognition and legitimacy. When I heard this, I knew there was no hope. So I packed my bags and left.

Had the parallel and secret Oslo peace negotiations been exposed, we could have avoided more than twenty years of hardship for the Palestinians living in the shadow of a false hope as Israel continued to colonise the land with impunity while assuming a peace-loving stance.

Having left Washington, I remained intrigued by the difference in attitude to the law taken by the two sides. I began exploring what I called the legal narrative of both. As I understand it, a legal narrative is how a people tell the story of their right to land, nationhood or resources using the symbolic language of law. A legal narrative is by necessity a construction. For it to stand it must have consistency and its own internal logic. It must also have external reference points to which others can relate. And it must be communicable.[2]

In the occupied territories Israel has mainly expressed its narrative through military orders which it wants to keep intact. As for the Palestinian leadership, their thinking on legal matters has been characterised by a search for absolutes, as is evident in the excessive importance they have attached to the recognition of the PLO, believing that if Israel were to recognise the PLO they would be recognising its programme of self-determination as well. It is also characterised by being abstract: the leadership have failed to take into account the changing legal reality and shifting ground over which negotiations have been conducted, and to anticipate the legal case of the other side, leaving them unable to respond adequately to it.

Elements of the narrative of this new period in the PLO struggle, characterised by agreeing to negotiations with Israel, can be traced to the meeting of the Palestinian National Council in Algiers on 15 November 1988, when the PLO recognised the need for an international conference whose aims would include the 'annulment of all measures of annexation and appropriation and the removal of settlements'. Alas, they failed to devise a strategy for achieving this key goal. Instead, the 1993 Declaration of Principles and the 1995 Interim Agreement reached between Israel and the PLO through the Oslo negotiations provided that the military orders were to remain in force. Though undeclared, what was in fact being preserved was the system of apartheid.

The different approaches of the two sides to the law cannot alone explain the dismal failure of the PLO in conducting negotiations with Israel. Another reason for this failure is that the leadership outside the occupied territories did not recognise or understand the nature of the struggle of those of us living under Israeli rule, just as we had failed to understand the struggle of Salim Dao and those who stayed in Israel after 1948. It seemed that the entire experience and struggle of the Palestinian people under occupation meant little to Palestinians living elsewhere, and so no lessons were learned. The dominance of one kind of struggle, that of the glamorous, if often doomed, *fedayeen* in the camps, prevailed at the expense of all others. This was certainly not because of a dearth of reporting from Palestinian organisations in the occupied territories.

I wonder if the reports we wrote in Ramallah at the human rights organisation Al-Haq, the Palestinian affiliate of the International Commission of Jurists, were ever accorded serious consideration by the leadership outside the occupied territories. Did our leaders, for example, take note of our study of Israel's Road Plan 50 of 1984?[3] This was a comprehensive reorganisation of roads in the West Bank aiming to link Israeli settlements, already built or planned, to each other and to Israel, bypassing Palestinian towns and villages. In the West Bank we succeeded in forming a national committee to challenge the plan, both as a whole and in its various sectors, by submitting hundreds of objections. We also suggested that the plan be challenged at the international level and recommended that the opinion of the International Court of Justice at The Hague be sought. We made sure that this study reached the PLO, but we never got any response from them. Perhaps I was naive to expect that legal resistance to the road plan stood any chance against the much more heroic armed struggle. When the leadership refused to listen to those of us in the occupied territories, I could hear the hollow echo of what we in the West Bank had said of the 1948 Arabs and our refusal to listen to them.

At this time I began noticing how the Israeli settlers were carefully planting trees, planning their settlements and landscaping their surroundings – hardly measures that suggested these were temporary establishments. The results are evident today. The Israelis have organised their presence on our land for their own use and enjoyment in the best possible manner. They also encourage their young- sters to hike in the land and get to know it. Nothing compa- rable was encouraged by our leaders. Now Israeli children know our land better than many Palestinians know it: its springs, its hills and wadis, to which they have given Jewish names. This difference in familiarity is compounded by increased restrictions on access to the land. A young man from the village of Lubban who is studying in Ramallah told me how he always used to visit the village spring when he went home. Now the nearby settlers have stopped the villagers from reaching the spring. He said he feared that the new generation would not even have memories of one of the village's important natural sites. When PLO leaders first returned after the Oslo Accords were signed in September 1993, many of them were shocked by the presence and degree of development of the Jewish settle- ments, their surprise betraying their failure to compre- hend. This had terrible consequences. For example, the occupied West Bank included a good part of the Dead Sea, with its potentially highly beneficial tourism and mineral extraction industries. But the Oslo deal severed the connec- tion between this important body of water and the Pales- tinians, who have had no access to it for the past twenty years.

It might be said that, twenty years after they were signed, the Oslo Accords are now part of history. The harm they did to the cause of peace has become well known. But the difference between the two sides in their approach to law and politics that led to the disastrous deal in Oslo persists in the case of Jerusalem. Throughout the Accords, Israel was careful to keep Jerusalem out of the negotiations. As a result the Palestinian Authority has never exercised any authority there. After the 1967 war Israel annexed East Jerusalem and its environs without once using the word annexation.

To oppose this annexation, the Palestinian and Jordanian leaderships ordered the Palestinian residents of the city to boycott municipal elections. There is no doubt that Israel's unilateral annexation was illegal under international law, and that by voting in the municipal elections the Palestinian sector of the city could be seen as legitimising this illegal action. Almost half a century later, the boycott has never been re-evaluated and the Jerusalem Palestinians have been left hostage to full Israeli rule, even though they constitute 38 per cent of the total population of Jerusalem. Could it have been otherwise without offering legitimacy to the annexation? By not allowing them to vote, Israel was given the greatest gift, free of charge. The Jerusalem Palestinians are left paying heavy taxes to the Israeli municipality while having no voice and no representation. Not surprisingly, discrimination against them is immense, whether in infrastructure, education, municipal services or economic prospects.

The PLO had no vision when attempting to counter Israeli actions in Jerusalem. While the Palestinians were adhering to the strictures of international law, right-wing Israeli groups were pursuing concrete plans to make the city Jewish and break down any continuity of Arab presence in East Jerusalem, which Palestinians want as their future capital. They could have empowered the substantial Palestinian presence in the city in a number of ways, but, blinded by fear of losing the reins of power, they were and continue to be willing to sacrifice the welfare of some 275,800 Palestinians.

After forty-five years of Israeli rule, Jerusalem has become a city organised, run and designed for the sole benefit and prosperity of its Israeli residents, with only a small area, a ghetto of sorts, left for the disenfranchised Palestinian residents.[4]

According to the leader of the settlers from the illegal settlement of Ofra near Ramallah, Pinchas Wallerstein, 'We built a splendid project ... In the last quarter of the twentieth century we did in Samaria [south of the West Bank] what Labor did in the Valley of Harod in the first quarter of the twentieth century.'[5]

If being in the vanguard pushing their government to follow is indeed the settlers' logic, it does not apply to East Jerusalem, where the government needed no pushing: settling in the expanded areas of East Jerusalem has been official policy right from the start. But the consequences are felt not only by the Arab Christian and Muslim population. In attempting to turn the Holy City into an exclusively Jewish enclave, the tolerance of Christians and Muslims, who also have legitimate claims to the city, is being stretched to the limit. It remains to be seen whether there will be stronger and more effective resistance to Israeli policy towards Jerusalem, especially if, as they have been threatening, extreme Jewish settlers bring down the Dome of the Rock, the third most sacred site for Muslims. It must be said here that, despite massive pressure and lobbying by Israel on successive US governments, the United States has still not moved its embassy from Tel Aviv to Jerusalem.

❧

The case of Jerusalem as an example of the inability of Palestinians to devise practical solutions through legal mechanisms stands in stark contrast to Israeli tactics. Israel never declared that it was annexing the West Bank and yet to all intents and purposes it has done exactly that. Compare this with the Palestinian struggle to win nominal recognition at the UN for the State of Palestine in 2012 when the Palestinian Authority has no sovereignty over any part of Palestine and no control over the borders. This illustrates the two ways of struggling: Israel's from below by administrative means and actions, and the PLO's by abstract formulae that sound robust but are almost empty of meaning. Sometimes the Palestinian struggle to embody the nominal, virtual acquisition of a state is undertaken in physical terms, such as the current construction in Ramallah of a million-dollar presidential palace for visiting heads of state coming to pay homage to the putative head of a state yet to be born.

After the Oslo deal was signed I spent some time writing about the different approaches to law of the two peoples. In 1997 I published *From Occupation to Interim Accords*, viewing and analysing the Oslo Accords in a legal context.[6] In a review of the book for the newspaper *Al Hayat* Edward Said, who had contributed a foreword, described what I was doing as a post-mortem. The die was cast; it was too late. My experience of working with the leadership had taught me that there was no role for a legal adviser, or indeed legal strategies, in the way that Palestinian politics was conducted. The role of the intellectual had changed, as had that of the human rights activist. Now that the Oslo Accords had restructured the occupation, it was no longer possible to sustain the belief that occupation could be brought to an end by documenting the violations of the occupier and exposing their effect on the 'protected population' suffering under a brutal occupation. Legal remedies for resisting the occupation also became subject to political negotiations between the Palestinian Authority and Israel. The PA's heavy dependence on Israel has meant that Israeli pressure can succeed in deterring the PA, for example, from joining the International Criminal Court and holding Israeli officials liable for the crimes they have committed against the Palestinian people. Instead of liberation we have ended up with a quasi-state where all powers are concentrated in the hands of one man, Mahmoud Abbas, the very same man who negotiated and signed the Oslo Accords.

Even after accepting the defeat and documenting how it came about, there was no respite, but instead an unsettling continuity in the experience of those who have been following Israeli settlement methods. Perhaps there can never be any respite under occupation.

In the summer of 2013, while reading a report of a land case, I saw the name of an Israeli lawyer I had encountered professionally years ago. In the cases I had been defending he'd pleaded before the military court that any land with a certain weed (called *natsh*) growing on it was obviously uncultivated and therefore public land. From the recent report I realised that he was still employing the same spurious legal tactics to defend the confiscation of Palestinian land, and still getting the same level of assistance from the Israeli Civil Administration, that he had been getting before the Oslo Accords. The similarities with those earlier cases were staggering. They included the use of fake documents in the name of a settler-created company – called no other than Al-Watan (The Homeland) – to register land near the illegal settlement of Ofra, bypassing a law that only a local company can buy land in the territory. In 1988 the Palestinian owner of the land in question had built a two-storey house on it. In 2003 this family came home one evening to discover that the locks on their house had been replaced and a Torah institute specialising in religion and finance had moved in. Both their house and the land around it had been taken and a new fence put up, with guard dogs to prevent them from even approaching. It took ten years for the District Court in Jerusalem to decide that the land sale was forged. Ten days after this court ruling, the head of the Central Command of the Israeli Army signed an order appropriating the house. After the family's victory in the case their lawyer sardonically commented, 'It took the family ten years of legal battles to win the case, but it is still unable to reach the "promised land".'[7] The case had all the elements of the pre-Oslo past: the Civil Administration helping the settlers, a collaborator recruited to carry out illegal practices, and the courts, both military and civil, in Israel showing bias and failing to assist the Arab claimant. Only this time everything was taking place under the noses of the Palestinian Authority, which had dismally failed to protect a Palestinian family against the illegal practices of Jewish settlers.

I was reminded of the words of Aharon, the settler from Ofra: 'We are not depriving you of anything. The more settlements the more progress. How can that be bad for you?'

4

2003: THE WALL

'In our time, political speech and writing are largely the defence of the indenfensible.'

George Orwell, *Politics and the English Language*

The 1967 June War, which is commonly called the Six Day War, did not last six days. The West Bank was taken in less than three, with little fighting between the Israeli and the Jordanian armies, the latter the only force defending the area. Israeli soldiers almost walked straight through. The Israeli Army did not need heroes to control Palestinian residents, who were already thoroughly demilitarised by the Jordanian regime. The ease with which the Israelis acquired the land has had dire consequences for them as well as for us Palestinians, and yet it might prove to be Israel's undoing.

Israel chose the name the Six Day War, thus giving the war biblical overtones. Just as God created the world in six days, so Israel took the West Bank and the other occupied territories in six days (no doubt resting on the seventh).

From then on more biblical allusions followed. Four months after the occupation began the West Bank was renamed 'Judea and Samaria', in an effort to seal its fate as a historical part of the State of Israel, and indeed of biblical Israel. A few months into the occupation the building of Jewish settlements started, and it has been escalating ever since. Settlement building became more intense after Israel signed the Oslo Accords in 1993. It was intended to give a clear message to the Palestinians, and to the world as a whole, that Israel, which is yet to determine its borders, considers all those undefined, borderless areas occupied in 1967 as its God-given territory – territory that it is unwilling to part with whatever the world thinks and whatever the applicable stipulations in international law prohibiting an occupier from settling its own people in occupied territory.

After 1967, there were Israeli voices inside and outside Israel warning of the dire consequences to the country of not ending the occupation soon. The strongest and most profound of these belonged to the late Yeshayahu Leibowitz, one of Israel's most brilliant scholars. He warned his countrymen that, taken to its logical conclusion, the occupation of the Palestinians would mean 'concentration camps would be erected by the Israeli rulers' and 'Israel would not deserve to exist, and it will not be worthwhile to preserve it'. He feared the ascendancy of right-wing, religious Jewish nationalists and warned that 'religious nationalism is to religion what National Socialism was to socialism'.

In a 1968 essay entitled 'The Territories', Leibowitz described what he thought the future would look like:

> The Arabs would be the working people and the Jews the administrators, inspectors, officials, and police – mainly secret police. A state ruling a hostile population of 1.5 to 2 million foreigners would necessarily become a secret-police state, with all that this implies for education, free speech and democratic institutions. The corruption characteristic of every colonial regime would also prevail in the State of Israel. The administration would suppress Arab insurgency on the one hand and acquire Arab Quislings on the other. There is also good reason to fear that the Israel Defense Force, which has been until now a people's army, would, as a result of being transformed into an army of occupation, degenerate, and its commanders, who will have become military governors, resemble their colleagues in other nations.[1]

But the Israeli government took no heed. Nor did it give serious consideration to offers of peace negotiations coming from the Arab side.

Immediately after the 1967 war, and before a single Jewish settlement had been established, my father and a group of some fifty Palestinian leaders made a proposal to the Israeli government for the resolution of the conflict that included (and I quote from the document I typed for him and he presented to the government) the following:

• The formation of an independent Palestine State

to be admitted as a member state in the United Nations.

- The territorial limits of the Palestine State shall be along the lines of the 1947 Partition Scheme with such necessary modifications as may be agreed upon by further negotiations.
- The Old City of Jerusalem surrounded by the ancient walls shall be under the joint sovereignty of the State of Israel and Palestine and ruled in accordance with a special agreement to secure free access to all Holy places.
- The capital of the Palestine State to be the Arab section of Jerusalem.
- Economic and non-aggression treaties shall be concluded between the two states.
- The independence and territorial boundaries of the Palestine State shall be guaranteed by the United Nations.
- Subject to any agreement as may be reached between the two states under the economic treaty referred to above: all rights of Palestinians in movable and immovable properties existing at the termination of the Mandate in both states shall be settled by mutual agreement. In case of dispute, however, such rights shall be settled in accordance with the principles laid down in the UN resolution of 12 December 1949.

Not only did local Palestinian leaders offer Israel peace, but so did King Hussein of Jordan. Yet faced with two actual options, Israel deferred making a decision. According to the

Israeli historian Avi Raz, author of *The Bride and the Dowry*, a scrupulous analysis of the first two years of the Israeli occupation after 1967, Israel did not want to give up any territory. Instead, it resorted to delaying tactics, which, Raz argues, later developed into a foreign policy of deception, claiming to want peace but arguing that there was no one to negotiate with.[2] Over time, there has been no change in this policy.

❧

In 1984 my father was murdered by a collaborator working for Israel. Much as we tried to bring the murderer to justice, we failed. The authorities in Israel preferred to protect the collaborator (who later died in a drug-related murder) than punish the murderer of a man of peace. This cynicism and refusal to recognise Palestinians whatever their views has also remained unchanged.

I wrote about my father and his tragic death, and the failure of Israel's justice system to pursue the case, in my 2009 book *Strangers in the House.* I was particularly pleased when this book was translated into Hebrew and became available to the Israeli public. I believed that by bringing this tragedy to their attention and showing how there are those among them responsible for favouring a murderer over an educated, peace-seeking man, some readers would express shame or contrition. But there was very little of that. It would appear that for the majority in Israel, sensitivity towards Palestinians has been blunted and obliterated.

Perhaps this is due to the repeated message they receive that they are the greatest and only victims. Adla Naser, a student at Birzeit University, examined the print editions of two Israeli dailies, *Haaretz* and the *Jerusalem Post*, between 20 October and 20 November 2013. During this period Jewish settlers committed thirty-two attacks of various types against Palestinians. Yet the English edition of *Haaretz* published only five items on the issue, while the *Jerusalem Post* published just one. In the same period *Haaretz* published twenty-one items on events that the paper described as anti-Semitic and the *Jerusalem Post* published twenty-nine.[3]

Much is known about the material suffering the Israeli occupation has caused, but there is little acknowledgement of its psychological impact. Like thousands of others, my mother lived with her tragic loss to the very last day of her life, needing to have certainty concerning who killed her husband but denied even this cold comfort.

In 2002 Israel began building a wall to separate Israel and the Palestinians. But rather than follow the 1967 border, a large proportion of the wall has been built inside the West Bank, annexing over 10 per cent of the West Bank to Israel. In an Orwellian twist, Israel calls this four-metre-high concrete wall a fence, and in doing so misappropriates the poet Robert Frost's line about good fences making good neighbours. In separating the Palestinian community from their fellow Palestinian neighbours, the wall is a bold symbol of the hegemony of the Israeli side, its hunger for annexing more Palestinian land and exerting more control over the Palestinian population. As Edward Said said early in 2003, 'Building walls ... is a kind of folly that ought to be exposed for exactly what it is, namely a delusion that can neither be made fully to work in theory or in practice. Ignorance of the other is not a strategy for survival.'[4] Among the wall's various purposes is to provide further occasions for Israel to grant permits selectively for Palestinians to cross it, rewarding those whom the Israeli authorities want to favour. They used to do this through the granting of telephone lines or driving licences, but now, having transferred many such functions to the PA, Israel has had to create new restrictions in order to exercise the power of giving, or withholding, favours.

In his documentary film *Infiltrators*, shown in Ramallah in the summer of 2013, the Palestinian artist Khaled Jarrar films Palestinians 'infiltrating' into their own territory, climbing over the wall to cross from one part of the West Bank to another in order to get to work, and in a few cases to Jerusalem to pray, receive medical treatment or visit relatives. It was painful to watch.

The Qasaba Theatre in Ramallah, where it was showing, was full. Many in the audience were middle-class people who for one reason or another – either they had money to spend in Israel or they were doing business with Israelis – could get permits to travel to Jerusalem without the hassle and danger of having to infiltrate. And there we all sat, watching without shedding a tear for our destitute fellow Palestinians, mainly working-class people seeking jobs, who had to go through the hazards and humiliation of climbing over that detestable wall. Was it voyeurism? What sort of people have we become that we can sit so passively and watch a film about our people's suffering that was devoid of redemption or relief? What has become of us? The film reminded me of Salim Dao's play, when he recounted how he felt about his fellow villagers becoming infiltrators as they tried to return to their own village. But now our world has shrunk even further. Not only is the region split into countries, but what is left of Palestine is further fragmented by checkpoints and stretches of wall, turning Palestinians attempting to cross over to East Jerusalem into criminals.

As in Salim Dao's play, the travails of the infiltrators were relieved by humour. Before climbing the ladder up the four-metre wall, one of them chuckles and asks, 'Do you think we'll be on Al Jazeera TV tonight?' Another, whose house borders the wall, painted his stretch white and then trained a creeper to climb over it, adding some greenery to mitigate its ugliness. He also planted trees all along its path.

How different and much more satisfying it was to have watched, a few weeks earlier, a German film, *The Promise*, also about a wall, but one that was ultimately brought down. Our own promise, to dismantle the wall that loops around our land, is still a long way from being fulfilled.

And how strange it is that our leadership neglects to do everything it can to enforce the 2004 decision of the International Court of Justice at The Hague calling for the dismantling of the sections of the wall built inside the Palestinian territories. Where we Palestinians succeed, it appears, is in making films and art installations out of our suffering, which we then present to the world. We sublimate our suffering into art. While our culture flourishes, we show every sign of having given up on politics. Is this healthy? *Infiltrators* was just a series of painful episodes of chase by and escape from soldiers and settlers, with no climax or even attempt at one. At no point in the film was there any reference to the Palestinian success in the fight against the wall at the Court of Justice.

In the course of 2013 there were numerous demonstrations against the wall in various parts of the West Bank. By the end of the year, with no steps taken towards pursuing the legal challenge against the wall, protesters began attempting to knock it down. This cannot be done in many parts, where it is difficult, dangerous or impossible to get close enough, but it was possible in Abu Dis, where the wall cuts through the town, obstructing the view of Jerusalem and its most distinctive landmark, the gold-plated Dome of the Rock. On 18 May 2013 demonstrators managed to open a four-metre-wide gap in the wall which they broke through. Hours after the action, Israeli border police blocked the opening with barbed wire. Similar incidents were reported in other parts of the West Bank. Since then there have been over twenty-two different incidents when holes were made in parts of the wall.

If Israelis hoped that Palestinians would reconcile themselves to living in the wall's shadow, they were mistaken because it's not happening.

Whenever I'm confronted by scenes of jostling chaos and confusion while trying to get through at 'checkpoints' – better described as places of sustained human misery – I remind myself of how it was at the end of the 1980s, and the solidarity of the first Intifada. Then, if one group – say, the taxi drivers – was punished or deprived of their rights, others would stand by them. With Oslo, much of that solidarity, and of the dream of an equitable society on which we hoped to build our state, has vanished and is hardly remembered. The main concern of most ordinary Palestinians is economic survival and, for the fortunate, consumerism. Plenty may still care, but few engage in politics. Many a nouveau-riche businessman has built an ostentatious dwelling perched on the hills, with no thought to minimise the damage done to our beautiful countryside. Perhaps the way society has developed is best illustrated by the manner in which people drive in my congested city, Ramallah: aggressively, at speed, rarely giving way to others. Everyone is vying for space in the small piece of land into which we have been crowded. The same is true in Nazareth, the only Arab city in Israel, where Arab citizens of Israel are packed in an area too small for their number, with Israeli planning authorities refusing to allow expansion. Similarly, Ramallah and other West Bank cities are circumscribed. The additional discrimination created by the Oslo Accords between the privileged and non-privileged was legislated in the Interim Agreement of 1995 between Israel and the PLO, in which, incredibly, an entire section was devoted to describing different categories of VIPs and the privileges each would enjoy, all of them to be granted – or withheld – by Israel, depending on how our esteemed leaders behaved. On more than one occasion Israel has threatened to withdraw these privileges, as happened after the breakdown of the negotiations sponsored by the US that began in July 2013. On that occasion Dr Mustafa Barghouti, a member of the Palestinian Legislative Council and the head of an independent political movement, Al Mubadara, called for a voluntary abandonment of these privileges.

A new vocabulary of oppression keeps creeping in and we adopt it, growing so accustomed to it that we stop noticing. With the construction of the wall came new terms, restrictions and requirements for obtaining yet more permits. Now there were 'seam zones' – closed military zones between the wall and the 1949 ceasefire line that constitutes the border between Israel and the West Bank. This area, comprising approximately 18 per cent of the West Bank, has given rise to a vast body of legal and bureaucratic arrangements. Entry to and exit from such areas by Palestinians now require 'proper permits'. There are also many checkpoints marking the internal borders between our towns and villages. To cross these numerous borders, one has to go through security checks similar to those at airports, complete with scanners and detection machines. The one in the Jordan Valley south of Beisan that marks the border between Israel and the West Bank is simply designated in Hebrew as *ma'abar* (crossing). At checkpoints placed at the entrance to Palestinian cities large red noticeboards proclaim in Arabic, Hebrew and English, 'You are entering Area A under the control of the Palestinian Authority', and go on to inform Israelis that the law forbids them from proceeding any further. The implication, which is not lost upon them, is that only upon entering Area A, which constitutes no more than about 18 per cent of the West Bank, are they entering a Palestinian area. All the rest of the West Bank is Israel, or, in the view of many, Eretz Israel (the biblical Land of Israel).

But how has Mandate Palestine been reduced to the tiny fragment now referred to as Area A?

The Declaration of the Establishment of the State of

Israel of 14 May 1948 states: '... by virtue of our natural and historic right and on the strength of the resolution of the United Nations General Assembly, [we] hereby declare the establishment of a Jewish state in Eretz-Israel, to be known as the State of Israel.'

The first annulment of 'Palestine' came in Article 15(a) of Law and Administration Ordinance No. 1 of 1948, which states: '"Palestine", wherever appearing in the law, shall henceforth be read as Israel.'

The State of Israel has yet to demarcate the exact borders of 'Eretz Israel', but even so the country is dotted with plenty of internal borders protected by large numbers of border police. Israelis and Palestinians have grown so used to their presence that few stop to question how this particular branch of the police came to have this name.

On 7 June 1967, when the Israeli Army occupied the West Bank of Jordan, along with East Jerusalem and the Gaza Strip, the army issued Proclamation No. 1, in which it declared that the army had 'entered' the area. The word occupied was never used. So much for international law and treaties.

Two sections of the area Israel entered were subject to outright annexation without using the term. The first was the area in the Latrun Salient where the three border villages of Beit Nuba, Emmaus and Yalu lay. Immediately after the occupation, these three border villages were razed to the ground, their inhabitants were forced to leave and the land was made part of Israel. A few years later Canada Park was established there, giving visitors the illusion that they were not crossing the Green Line into the West Bank.

On 27 June 1967, the Law and Administration Ordinance

was amended by the addition of Article 11B, which states that 'the law, jurisdiction and administration of the State shall extend to any area of Eretz Israel designated by the Government by order'.

This law was used to annex East Jerusalem, the second section, to Israel.[5] The 1980 Jerusalem Law declared Jerusalem to be the 'complete and united' capital of Israel. One cannot but wonder how a city becomes 'complete'. Not only have the two parts of the city (which are united only by name) become united by power of law, but the city came to be referred to as 'the eternal capital of Israel', thus making Jerusalem complete, united and eternal. As for those of us Palestinians living in the rest of the West Bank, we await our turn to be annexed. Naftali Bennett, Minister of the Economy, and his party, Habayit Hayehudi, are calling for the annexation of the Israeli settlements. Surely our turn will come, especially if the Israeli policy of encouraging Palestinians to leave reduces our numbers.

We have been given many names. In 1981, when the Israeli military established the 'Civil Administration', the area began to be referred to by Israelis and the media as the 'Administered Territories' or, for short, 'the territories'.[6] Until 1993 and the signing of the Oslo Accords, these designations applied to the entirety of the West Bank, less East Jerusalem. With Oslo, Palestine was reduced in the eyes of most Israelis to Area A, constituting 18 per cent of the whole of the West Bank, entry into which by Israelis was forbidden under Israeli law.

But the changes affected not only the territory, but also the Palestinians living there. Israel, which claims to aspire towards making peace with us, has come to refer to us as a 'demographic threat'. Reconciliation between neighbours is rarely invoked by Israel as the motivation for making peace; rather, it is getting rid of the Palestinian population living in 'Eretz Israel', thereby removing the biggest threat to Israel's existence as a Jewish state, that is upheld as the greatest benefit of peace.

Few seem to be aware that the real and much greater threat facing all of us, Israelis and Palestinians alike, is not demographic, but concerns a nuclear Middle East. In one of the longest examples of convoluted language, Israel has for decades been pursuing 'a policy of ambiguity' regarding whether or not it is in possession of nuclear arms, even when it is an open secret that the nuclear reactor at Dimona in the Negev Desert has been producing nuclear warheads. According to a recent report, Israel has eighty of the world's 16,300 nuclear warheads.[7] And yet attempts by the Arab League to have Israel join the Nuclear Non-Proliferation Treaty and make its nuclear facilities subject to international supervision are repeatedly defeated by member states of the International Atomic Energy Agency. The last such attempt was in September 2014.[8]

Talks are proceeding regarding Iran's nuclear programme. It is to be hoped that these will succeed in restraining Iran from developing a nuclear bomb. For the time being, Israel remains the only nuclear power in the region. It is also the only country that possesses chemical weapons. Its determination not to ratify the Chemical Weapons Convention has not changed, even though the destruction of the Syrian arsenal of such weapons has made substantial progress.

Egypt has been calling on the UN to hold a conference to

rid the region of nuclear weapons. The latest such call was made on 7 December 2013, when the UN General Assembly adopted two draft resolutions sponsored by Egypt to create a nuclear-free Middle East. Whether or not anything will come of this remains to be seen.

Meanwhile, in Haifa, a conference was held on 5 December 2013 that advocated a Middle East without nuclear or other weapons of mass destruction. One of the organisers, a former Knesset member and a Palestinian, Issam Makhoul, said, referring to Israel's decision not to take part in the Helsinki Conference that met in 2012, 'If Israel won't go to Helsinki, Helsinki will come to Israel.' The conference was an attempt to open a debate in Israel on nuclear weapons.

So far, the presence of the nuclear reactor at Dimona remains shrouded in official secrecy and Israel continues to refuse to accede to the Nuclear Non-Proliferation Treaty. As a result, no international inspection of the facility can take place. This puts all of us who live in the region under threat. What if this old reactor is unsafe? Where and how is the nuclear waste disposed of? Has the reactor been strengthened against a major earthquake (one has struck the region every hundred years or so and is now overdue)? No one knows the answers to these questions.

❧

A photographer friend of mine, Bassam Almohor, had an idea for a book. He walked up and down Ramallah's Main Street, his camera against his thigh, taking photographs of people passing by. He then did the same along Jaffa Road in West Jerusalem, a predominantly Jewish neighbourhood.

When he looked at both sets of photographs he was struck by how similar the two sets of people are. You could hardly tell Arab from Jew, he told me.

It is not only the faces that are similar but also the languages of the two sides, Arabic and Hebrew. And yet, according to the Israeli columnist Yossi Klein:

> being raised on a certain image of the Arab did something to us: Today it is hard to find Arabic speakers in Israel who are not Arabs or who were not born in a Muslim country. Ninety percent of the Arabs in Israel speak Hebrew, while only 3 percent of Israeli-born Jews speak Arabic. Last year [2012] only some 2,000 Jewish high-school students took the matriculation exam in the language of 20 percent of their country's residents. The teenagers who took that test in Arabic did not see it as a bridge: They saw it as a weapon, and most of them, presumably, were inducted into Unit 8200.[9]

A number of Arabic words are now commonly used by Hebrew speakers: for example, *ahlan*, which is a popular greeting like hello in English, and *walla*, which means 'by Allah' or 'by God'. Fewer Hebrew words are used by Arabic speakers. With the exception of *yom yom*, meaning daily, and *ramzon* (from the Hebrew word *ramzor*) for traffic lights, most of the Hebrew words that have entered daily parlance have a military or security connotation, such as *makhsom* for checkpoint, which is given the Arabic plural form *makhaseem*, and *makhsheer* for walkie-talkie.

Often Arabic words are turned into swear words: *shabab-*

nikkim is pejorative Hebrew slang for right-wing extremist youths from ultra-Orthodox homes who are on the fringes of Orthodox society. They are often yeshiva dropouts who have picked up some of the anti-Arab views that can be found even in certain rabbinical writings. The word is rooted in the Arabic *shabab* (youth). In Israeli society the word is associated with stone-throwing hooligans. In the various institutions that teach the language to new immigrants, the accent used is European not Middle Eastern. This helps to distinguish Hebrew speakers who are Arab from the non-Arabs. At checkpoints and in airports, if the guard is confused he engages the person in conversation to find out from his accent whether or not he is Arab, so as to apply the rules for treating Arabs in such situations.

Perhaps the most cynical and convoluted exploitation of these similarities in looks and language is when they are used by Israeli operatives called *must'arab'een* (Arabised; acting or pretending to be Arabs) who mingle with Palestinians to identify and then arrest or kill activists. When soldiers masquerading as Arabs were attacked last autumn by settlers in the southern part of the West Bank near the village of Susia, politicians in Israel criticised the army's use of these lookalikes and excused the actions of the settlers because, when they attacked the soldiers, they 'believed they were terrorists'.

On 26 August 2014, members of the Knesset from the Israeli parties Yisrael Beiteinu (Israel is Our Home), Likud and Habayit Hayehudi submitted a bill that called on the government to rescind the status of Arabic as an official language in Israel. They did this in the name of greater 'social cohesion' in the country.

In September 2014, when Israel's Population, Immigration and Borders Authority released its annual statement for the Jewish New Year, included was a list of the most popular baby names in Israel. Whereas in fact Mohammed, an Arab name, came top, the official list hid this fact, claiming that the most popular names were the Jewish ones Yosef, Daniel and Uri.

❧

In the summer of 1998, the Israel Museum in Jerusalem put on an intriguing exhibition entitled *To the East: Orientalism in the Arts in Israel*. It showed the shift among Zionist immigrants from being enamoured with the exotic Orient to an almost complete disregard in the post-state period. According to the curator, Yigal Zalmona, 'The East was and remains foreign to Israelis – whether to those who wanted to touch it, become a part of it and internalise it, or (all the more so) to those who wanted nothing to do with it.'[10]

Much as Israel has tried to keep separate the Palestinian population in Israel from that in the occupied territories, the commonality of experience is bringing the two populations closer together. The fact that Salim Dao, a Haifa-born Palestinian actor, could perform his play successfully in Ramallah means that, despite their significantly different experience of the Nakba, Palestinians from the 1948 area are finally able to tell their story to a sympathetic and understanding audience in Palestinian areas occupied in 1967. This empathy has been fostered by the shared experience of Israel's policies towards its Palestinian population on both sides of the border, whether with regard to denial of rights over their land or systemic discrimination and economic strangulation. In essence, the legal ploys used on both sides of the border were the same. But whereas our world in the West Bank shrank gradually, those Palestinians who stayed on their land in 1948 had the bizarre experience of going to sleep in one country only to wake up in another. The new country denied that there was anything there before it was established, while insisting that its own history in the land extended back thousands of years.

Because peace was not achieved in 1967, Israel was able to continue with its occupation of Palestinian lands and use the same tactics against the Palestinians living inside the 1948 borders as it had earlier. Over time, the similarities in our experiences have only increased. Even the ethnic cleansing Israel was guilty of in 1948, which we call our Nakba, is continuing in the territories occupied in 1967. Israel implements policies in the territories it occupied that aim to make the life of Palestinians living on their land so intolerable that they decide to leave. My own experience of life in the occupied West Bank leads me to believe that Israel has not stopped trying to drive the Palestinians out of their land through various practices and administrative manoeuvres. Since 1967, 14,000 Palestinians in East Jerusalem have had their status as permanent residents of Israel revoked. Tens of thousands wait to be allowed to rejoin families in the West Bank and the Gaza Strip. In January 2012 the Israeli High Court agreed to continued suspension of family reunification.[11] Israel remains in control of the borders as well as the population register even in areas under the Palestinian Authority's control. Without Israeli approval, Palestinians do not have the right to reside in their own country, nor can they visit it.

So many of the Jerusalem friends with whom I grew up have for one reason or another lost their right of residency and can no longer live here. Among them is Khalil Mahshi, a school friend who was born and raised in Jerusalem but who, after an illustrious career with UNESCO in Paris, was deprived of his Jerusalem identity card and is denied the right to retire to his home city. He was able to afford to buy a flat in the South of France, but, as he has written to me:

We now live in France, where we know almost no one and do not have friends. This is extremely difficult. It is a beautiful city and region – paradise! However, we miss our friends back home. Memories are what makes us homesick, really. In Palestine, we feel loved and appreciated. In France, very few know that we exist and, maybe more importantly, what we stand for. We miss this feeling. Our children are scattered in different parts of the world. We have become a family without a clear home or base.

Reporting on his last interview with the Israeli authorities, he said:

The lady from the Ministry of Interior who interviewed me is much younger than I am. She was not born when I was daily walking through the streets of the Old City to go to school and come back home. At the end of the interview, she asked me if there was anything I would like to add or ask. I asked if the Ministry would allow me to die in my country and be carried to my grave and buried by my friends and relatives rather than being carried and buried by a professional company in France, where almost nobody knows me. She did not understand what I meant by my question. She asked me if I had health problems, and was surprised when I replied that my health was excellent!

Such is the despair of Palestinian refugees and deportees about ever setting foot on the soil of their country that in Hebron, whose people are famous for their entrepreneurial spirit, a shoemaker has produced a shoe that contains a small amount of Palestinian soil in the sole.

5

2013: THE BEGINNING OF THE END OF NEGOTIATIONS

'We could not have found peace unless the desire for it was already here.'

Colum McCann, *TransAtlantic*

No language of peace and reconciliation has emerged from the long and painful process of negotiations that has been proceeding on and off now for over twenty-five years. Instead, what we have seen is a restatement of the relationship between Israel and the Palestinians, with Israel, the more powerful side, dictating its terms.

The test of a successful peace treaty is whether it really does mark the end of a relationship between two sides that has been characterised by violence and ushers in a period of peace when differences can be settled through negotiation and there are genuine grounds for anticipating better times for all. Violence should be taken to include the forceful usurpation of the land of one side to build settlements there for the exclusive benefit of the other.

The Oslo Accords of 1993 obviously did not pass the test. Pronouncements such as those made on 13 September, in the Preamble to the Declaration of Principles on Interim Self-Government Arrangements, that 'The Government of the State of Israel and the PLO team ... representing the Palestinian people, agree that it is time to put an end to decades of confrontation and conflict, recognize their mutual legitimate and political rights, and strive to live in peaceful coexistence and mutual dignity and security and achieve a just, lasting and comprehensive peace settlement and historic reconciliation through the agreed political process', were no substitute for action.

Almost everything that followed belied this stated intention. The Israeli military merely transferred to the Palestinian Authority those legal arrangements it had put in place to ensure the fulfilment of the overall objectives of the occupation. These included the effective annexation of large parts of the occupied territories and all the restrictions on Palestinian civil life that prevent it from developing in any way that is not to Israel's liking or that works against Israel's long-term policies.

What should be obvious is the limits of power. A new relationship between the two sides based solely on the power relationship between them only perpetuates the old relationship where violence was the common language, regardless of how it was exhibited and expressed – whether by killing, maiming or stealing land. For things to be different, the majority of Israelis and Palestinians have to truly believe that peaceful negotiations can change matters fundamentally. This faith, which was prevalent before the Oslo Accords, was profoundly shaken by the negotiations that led to their adoption. The failure to achieve a just settlement only strengthened the rejectionists and the proponents of violence.

When I first investigated the difference in approach between Israel and the PLO, I became envious of the legal experts Israel had at its disposal. However, in time I came to realise that they have ultimately done Israel a great disservice, helping it to avoid the peace it desperately needs. They and their leaders should have acted less like lawyers and more like patriots.

One of the consequences of the Oslo Accords was that most of the military orders that encapsulate the Israeli language for controlling Palestine remained in place. This was thanks in large part to the advice from the Israeli legal counsels. This meant that the Palestinian legal narrative was given a severe and possibly fatal blow, while the Israeli narrative was confirmed and promoted as the only official version. The common language of progressives on both sides was lost. The Declaration of Principles of 1993 was falsely hailed as marking a new phase in the relationship between Israel and the PLO. While all the features of the occupation and all the effects of war remained, peace was proclaimed and the handshake between Arafat and Rabin on the White House lawn was shown repeatedly around the world. Subsequently, as we have seen, words such as 'infiltrator' and concepts such as 'security' have assumed a whole new meaning.[1]

Despite their failure, the Oslo Accords remain the binding agreement that has so far not been replaced or annulled. It was the Oslo Accords that created the Palestinian Authority, which continues to exist, exercising those powers and observing the limits imposed by the 1993 and 1995 agreements.

But the Oslo Accords were never intended as a final agreement. They were to be an interim phase, followed by a final status agreement negotiated by Israel and the PLO. Israel interpreted the Accords as giving it more land for settlements and proceeded to convince its population of this, as is evident from the large increase in settlement building after they were signed. Palestinians thought the Accords would lead to a fully independent state. The European Union supported the Palestinians, providing funds to help the Palestinian Authority build the institutions of state (the judiciary, local councils and the security forces). This support went ahead as the territory left to the Palestinians on which to build their state continued to diminish in size. The final status agreement has not happened yet and we remain at the interim stage, watching as more of our territory is being eaten away.

One of the terrible consequences of the Oslo Accords is that they allow Israel to believe that when its army redeploys from an area that is then transferred to the Palestinian Authority it is 'giving' something to the Palestinians rather than fulfilling obligations imposed by international law. As such, Israel then begins to feel that it must take something in return, must bargain, must try to 'give' as little as possible. Israel has been known to bargain over the same thing three times, on each occasion winning more concessions.[2]

Among the benefits that Israel derived from the Oslo Accords was exemption from having to care for the welfare of the local population under occupation. It was mainly the EU that assumed this burden, justifying it as assistance to the Palestinian Authority (amounting to $25 billion from 1993 to 2012) to help it build the institutions needed for when the time came for Palestinians to govern themselves in a state of their own. But by March 2013, with the collapse of negotiations imminent once Israel had made it clear that it was not intending to recognise a separate Palestinian state, the EU was put in a dilemma. It was inconceivable that it would continue giving aid and in effect funding the occupation indefinitely. Brussels transferred more than £1.95 billion to the occupied territories between 2008 and 2012. At the same time, it was also aware that stopping aid would lead to the collapse of the PA, while the resulting impoverishment and destitution of the Palestinian population would in all likelihood lead to a third Intifada.

The latest attempt at replacing the Oslo Accords by another framework agreement began in earnest with high hopes under US sponsorship in July 2013. Let us review here the course of these negotiations and try to determine why they failed.

Perhaps the most fundamental reason for their failure derives from the policies put in place by Menachem Begin, Israel's prime minister at the time of the Camp David negotiations with Egypt in 1978. In 1979 Begin said that through the Jewish settlement project he wanted to make it politically impossible for any Israeli government to withdraw from the territories Israel had occupied in 1967. Danny Gutwein sheds light on how this process happened:

> The gradual liquidation of the Israeli welfare state and the privatization and commercialization of its services have expanded the economic gaps and exacerbated the social inequality that hurt mainly the lower classes. Thus, the liquidation of the welfare state has turned the occupation of the Palestinian Territories and its byproducts – in particular the settlements and the split of the Israeli labor market – into a compensatory mechanism that has protected the Israeli lower classes from the detrimental impact of privatization. Privatization intensified the lower classes' bonds with the political Right, alienated them from the Left, and created the social and political basis for the perpetuation of the Occupation.[3]

Begin's Likud party aspired to give the Palestinian population a form of autonomy for themselves but not their land, with a strong local police force and no sovereignty. All of these objectives have now been achieved. The Palestinian Authority was established along the lines envisaged by Israel many decades ago and Israel now lives as a hostage to the settlers' lobby. Such a situation is not conducive to making peace. Not only are the settlers strong in the central government of Israel but they also have great leverage over the Israeli Civil Administration, which controls most of the territory of the West Bank. According to the State Comptroller's Report of July 2013, land use planning and construction for West Bank settlers is a free-for-all.

At the time of the first ever negotiations between Israel and its Palestinian neighbours, the Israeli government was headed by Yitzhak Shamir, who followed Begin's ideology and was no less obdurate. As a right-wing hawk, he was against the negotiations from the start. The tremendous efforts of James Baker, the US Secretary of State, threats of reducing US aid and incentives given to Israel succeeded in dragging the country to the peace conference held in Madrid in September 1991. The PLO was more supportive of the negotiations. The intransigent nature of the Israeli government at the start of the US-sponsored talks that began in July 2013 was not much different. The Israeli government was led by Prime Minister Benjamin Netanyahu, who also tried his best to stay away from the negotiations. This is understandable, since the make-up of his government, with three cabinet ministers living in illegal settlements in the occupied West Bank, makes it highly unlikely that it can offer any meaningful concessions to the Palestinians and survive.

Another similarity with earlier talks is that they were played out against a background of turmoil in the international arena. The Oslo Accords were negotiated after the fall of the Berlin Wall and the end of apartheid, not to mention the Soviet Union. The new initiative took place in a period of dramatic change and instability in the region, from Tunis to Iraq, and particularly in Syria. But where the first Palestinian Intifada had created an incentive for Israel to arrive at some political arrangement with the Palestinians, by the start of the July 2013 talks Israel's control of the occupied territories was complete.

There were other features of these talks that were

reminiscent of the negotiations that led to the signing of the Oslo Accords. Then the US had put pressure on the PLO and its chairman Yasser Arafat to accept the limited terms of the negotiations. The Americans did this by indicating to the PLO that its lease in Tunis was running out and it would have to find refuge elsewhere. They also showed signs of supporting its rival, Hamas, as well as holding high-level meetings with Faisal Husseini, the head of the Palestinian negotiating team in Washington, to indicate that they would support the creation of a leadership from within the occupied territories to replace the hegemony of the PLO there, a development that Arafat always dreaded. This was the stick. The carrot was an offer of financial support once the deal was signed. These tactics proved successful and Arafat was willing to sign. In the same way this time, the Europeans lent their support to US efforts by wielding the carrot and the stick against both sides.

For the Palestinians the stick took the form of threats by the EU to stop the funding that enabled the Palestinian Authority to continue to function and pay the salaries of its civil service. This threat also worked against Israel, which is being spared the expense of having to provide for the welfare of the population living under Israeli occupation, as is mandated in the Hague Regulations of 1907. Israel was also threatened with more European sanctions against the settlements if the negotiations failed.[4]

Meanwhile, some American Jewish supporters of Israel were adding their voice. At a meeting to discuss 'What it means to be pro-Israel in America', held in New York on 11 December 2013, Jeremy Ben Ami, leader of J Street (an American Jewish lobby created to foster a more open, honest discussion about Israel among American Jews), denounced the boycott of Israeli academic institutions earlier that year by the American Studies Association and said, 'The underlying issue continues to be whether Israel and the Palestinians will achieve a two-state solution.' Until then, he added, 'We can help the Israeli policy makers understand that this wave is coming, that Israel is headed towards international isolation, towards being a pariah state, not simply because there are anti-Semites in the world – though there are and always will be – but because of Israel's own policy of continuing occupation and the way Palestinians are treated in the 21st century.'[5]

The carrot dangled before the Israeli leadership took the form of promises of 'an unprecedented assistance package to Israel and the Palestinians, if the two parties sign a final-status agreement'.[6]

After 1993 and the success of the negotiations that led to the signing of the Oslo Accords, there was great excitement about the future and the Western world poured in a lot of money to distract the Palestinians by shifting the focus towards economic development. But soon the reality of the deal became evident and, despite the money, a people's rebellion in 2000 took the form of a second, and this time disastrous, violent Intifada which left the two sides further apart and the prospect of peace between them more distant than ever. As the US-led negotiations were taking place in 2013, many feared that the same might happen yet again, with a bad deal packaged to look attractive but delivering nothing.

But unlike on earlier occasions, these latest US-sponsored negotiations did not begin with much enthusiasm on either side. Indeed, I seemed to be among the very few who believed something might come of them. Israel agreed to participate to avoid looking as if it was doing nothing for peace. The talks took place behind closed doors between two hugely unequal sides. There was never any indication that they would be based on international law. One of the parties, Israel, controlled the very existence of the other, the Palestinian Authority, as well as most aspects of Palestinian life. Had there been a powerful third party invoking the Fourth Geneva Convention and taking seriously the enforcement mechanisms provided in that law, then Israel as an occupier would simply have had to withdraw and undo the consequences of its long-term illegal occupation. But the third party sponsoring these talks is biased towards one side. A month after the talks began in July 2013 there was still no agreement on the agenda. A survey conducted by the Israeli Democracy Institute and published by Reuters on 6 August 2013 found that most Israelis oppose withdrawing to pre-1967 ceasefire lines, even if land swaps to accommodate Jewish settlements were agreed to, and that 65.5 per cent of those questioned did not expect to see a peace deal within a year. Among Palestinians a poll conducted by the East Jerusalem-based Jerusalem Media and Communications Center found that 50 per cent considered peace talks with Israel a mistake. This has led a number of observers on both sides to note accurately that the most any Israeli leader is prepared to offer is less than the minimum that any Palestinian leader could ever accept. The distinction has to be made between a fully fledged peace and an interim settlement. The Israeli government, with the assistance of the Americans, seemed to be seeking the latter. Very often in the international media reference is made to 'resolving the dispute between Israel and the Palestinians'. By reducing a colonial occupation to a mere 'dispute', they fail to appreciate the magnitude of the conflict between the two sides.

And indeed language continues to reveal how censorious Israeli leaders were even of Palestinians' dreams. During the course of the negotiations a message sent by Prime Minister Benjamin Netanyahu to US Secretary of State John Kerry included a YouTube video of the popular Palestinian vocalist Mohammed Assaf, dubbed *mahboub el Arab* (beloved by the Arabs), who won first place in the popular TV contest *Arab Idol* and was later made a goodwill ambassador to UNRWA. In all the gloom of occupation and perpetual defeat, Assaf represented one bright spot, as his singing brought joy and happiness to many people. But the prime minister of Israel considered the way Assaf sang longingly about cities in Israel that were once Palestinian an incitement.

Israel's use of the security pretext has often led to absurd conclusions. To help the economy of Gaza by allowing its agricultural produce to reach the West Bank, Holland donated a scanner for containers to Israel. It hoped by doing so to provide Israel with a solution to its security concerns regarding exports from Gaza. But Israel still refused to allow the produce in. The Defence Ministry explained that, for security reasons, Israel wanted to isolate the West Bank from the Gaza Strip, and allowing goods from Gaza into the West Bank would contravene this policy. Palestinian officials had nothing to say on any of this.

❧

The power of the settlers' lobby has given rise in Israel to strange linguistic formulations. Thus, to calm opposition to the release of Palestinian prisoners in October 2013, one of the conditions agreed upon between Israel and the Palestinian Authority for renewing peace talks, the settlers called for an 'appropriate Zionist response' and persuaded the government to agree to the construction of some 5,000 new housing units in East Jerusalem and the West Bank. What bizarre logic this is, building more illegal settlements on occupied land to 'offset' the prisoner release. The PA condemned the move. It was like a molested person condemning his molesters. One wonders what this means and what effect Palestinian condemnation can have. Perhaps it would have been better for the Palestinians, who are impotent in the face of further Israeli construction on the West Bank, to have remained silent. While the peace talks were proceeding, Israel continued to prejudice their outcome by enlarging the settlements in the West Bank and the PA continued to issue condemnations.

Reviewing the pronouncements of the Israeli leadership during the time of the negotiations, compromise did not appear to be in the offing. This was why many anticipated that these talks were doomed. In a speech given to the Saban Forum at the Brookings Institute in Washington, DC, on 8 December 2013, the Israeli prime minister claimed, 'Few people still link the problems in the Middle East to the Israeli–Palestinian conflict', implying that it is not so important to resolve the conflict. He avoided the subject of negotiating borders by contending that 'the core of this conflict has never been borders and settlements. It's about one thing, the persistent refusal to accept the Jewish state in any border.' How strange to argue and try to convince the world that a state does not need to demarcate its borders, and that it can keep on expanding and still expect to have peace with its neighbours, whose lands are threatened by that expansion.

This denial of history is commonplace not only with the prime minister of Israel. In an interview he gave to the Israeli press on the eve of Independence Day, Shimon Peres, the former president of Israel, said:

> I remember how it all began. The whole state of Israel is a millimeter of the whole Middle East. A statistical error, barren and disappointing land, swamps in the north, desert in the south, two lakes, one dead and an overrated river. No natural resource apart from malaria. There was nothing here. And we now have the best agriculture in the world? This is a miracle: a land built by people.[7]

Almost all of the above is part of the myth Israel developed and constantly tries to market as truth. Malaria was beaten well before Israel was established, swamps were marshes that sustained a way of life for an entire group of Palestinian Arabs, and the Dead Sea is rich in resources. The biggest and most serious lie, however, is the oft-repeated claim that Palestine was an empty desert before the Jewish people came to it.

A more truthful picture of the reality is given in the 2011 film by Nabil Ayouch called *My Land*. It consists of two sets of interviews, one with Israelis and the other with Palestinians. The Israelis were mainly young men and women in their twenties. They lived on the same land where the Palestinians interviewees, all of whom had been forced out in 1948, had lived, sometimes in the same house. Most of them were born and grew up in these places and were viscerally attached to the land. They held nationalist and political views, lacked memory and lived in denial, even when in some cases they looked beyond the border to the places where the Palestinians had taken refuge. The Palestinians in refugee camps in Lebanon were among the most enthusiastic and hopeful that the Palestinian revolution would succeed in enabling them to return to their homes. Their present feelings about the state they are in, and the response to their suffering of the Israelis living in the places that had once belonged to them, were movingly portrayed in the film.

The film-maker was born in France in 1969 to a Moroccan Muslim father and a Jewish mother of Tunisian descent. He had carried out a number of interviews with Palestinian refugees in Lebanon and he showed them to the young Israelis. The result was a sort of conversation between protagonists who never meet.

However, conforming to the usual pattern, the Palestinians – the oppressed side – are not given a voice: the conversation in the film was one-sided. Whereas Ayouch showed the Israelis the interviews with the Palestinians, he did not show the Palestinians what the Israelis had said and how they described the places where they were living. And yet the range of responses from the young Israelis was surprising. Only a few repeated the tired old sentiments and beliefs that are usually put forward by Israel: that there was a war and the other side lost, that the Arab leaders told the Palestinians to leave and that it is the fault of the refugees for not making a better life for themselves. Most of those who were exposed to the lives and memories of the other side were visibly moved. Two opposing responses stand out. The first was from a young woman who simply brushed everything aside, saying that Israel is small and it is the only place for the Jewish people to live. The other was from a young woman who grew up in a mixed Arab-Jewish community in Haifa. When asked whether she thought the land was too small she said it was her belief that only the heart, not the place, was too small.

What was visually striking throughout the film was the beauty and openness of the places where the Israelis lived, in contrast to the cramped and miserable refugee camps where the Palestinians have been struggling to survive since their expulsion. In the film it appeared that the small screen of the portable computer on which the Israelis were watching the interviews with the Palestinians had brought that reality – not so distant, spatially or temporally – as close as possible. A few were in tears when they finished watching the interviews. Denial of past tragedies will not lead to forgiveness and peace. Perhaps shedding tears is not a bad place to start.

Sometimes tears come from unexpected quarters. Watching the film, I was reminded of the words of the mother of Israeli artist Dvora Morag, an Auschwitz survivor, who said, 'We can't take the apartment in Jaffa, because we can't do what they did to us.'[8] It's an equation that is still not accepted by a world that, on the whole, continues to base its support of Israel and its refusal to recognise the Nakba on the tragedy that befell the Jews in the Holocaust.

It is difficult to see how peace can come as long as Israeli leaders continue to hold on to and perpetuate a mythologised history of their country, refusing to recognise that there was a nation prospering there before and that to build their own state they had to replace this nation.

From Shimon Peres's unhelpful comment we come to Netanyahu's demand that the Palestinian Authority recognise Israel as a Jewish state as a precondition for continuing peace negotiations, a demand which hastened the suspension of those negotiations.

Some ten days before negotiations were called off, the Israeli historian and political commentator Zeev Sternhell wrote in *Haaretz*: 'The demand that the Palestinians recognize a Jewish state is no coincidence; it's not to be taken lightly. It's the way to demand that the Palestinians admit their historic defeat and recognize the Jews' exclusive ownership of the country.'

He concluded:

for Israel's leaders, the word 'agreement' means unconditional Palestinian surrender. For the Jews' exclusive right to the land to be complete and recognized, the Palestinians must accept their inferiority. This perception is anchored deep in the Israeli consciousness and is shared by the right, the center and the center-left, the towns in the country's outskirts and most residents of Greater Tel Aviv, the Labor Party and Likud. They all reject the principle of equal rights for the Arabs ...

So at the moment there is no chance to forge a majority for a fair agreement. Even if Likud miraculously splits in a move led by the prime minister – who would try to go down as a de Gaulle rather than as a son of Prof. Netanyahu – and the necessary majority is found, it won't be considered legitimate by large parts of the population. Nobody will have the courage to implement the new policy.

He then went on to outline how the right-wing Israelis view history:

In the eyes of the right, the Jewish people won a decisive victory when they occupied the country in a process that began with the First Aliyah – the immigration wave from 1882 to 1903 – and continues to this day. Its two high points were the War of Independence and the Six-Day War, both part of the sequence of settlement. In that sense there is no difference between the occupation of parts of the country before and after 1949, while the Green Line has no significance except for being a temporary cease-fire line.[9]

If further proof were needed that the current Israeli government is not interested in reaching an agreement, we need only consider the amount of land that has been confiscated since the start of the negotiations. A record 28,000 dunums (6,919 acres) were unilaterally declared 'state land' by Israel, using a legal ploy it has favoured for over three decades to take Palestinian land and designate it for the exclusive use of Jewish settlers.[10] In the nine months of the negotiations, the Israeli government constructed no fewer than 13,850 new housing units in the West Bank for Jewish settlers on the very territory that was the subject of the negotiations. And after all this Israel still claims that the violence is perpetrated by the Palestinian side.

This time round, the US had incorrectly read the situation. In 1991, the first Intifada had been raging and Israel wanted an end to it, so had an incentive to take part in negotiations. Now the Palestinians were defeated and Israel was riding high. The US tried to indicate with the EU that there would be consequences to a lack of agreement, but this did not work with Israel and the US seemed disinclined to use its considerable leverage over Israel. The US Secretary of State, John Kerry, who had started in July 2013 with the goal of reaching a full peace agreement between the Israelis and Palestinians within a period of nine months, was forced to announce the much-reduced objective of reaching a framework agreement and ultimately concluded with the hope of 'determining conditions for holding talks'. Throughout this period, as *Der Spiegel* reported on 3 August 2014, Israel was eavesdropping on Kerry. At the end of the nine months, on 8 April, by which time nothing had been achieved, the Secretary of State of the world's great superpower told the Senate Foreign Affairs Committee that Israel was refusing to release the last group of Palestinian prisoners it had promised to release at the start of the talks. 'And so,' he said, 'day one went by, day two went by, day three went by. And then in the afternoon, when they were about to maybe get there, 700 settlement units were announced in Jerusalem and, poof, that was sort of the moment. We find ourselves where we are.'

After nine agonising months of high expectations, feverish talk, dozens of meetings and phone calls between

John Kerry and Israeli and Palestinian leaders, the negotiations officially ended with a 'poof' rather than a peace agreement. Later, using flight terminology, Kerry would describe the talks as being in a holding pattern, while President Obama said they were at a pause. For his part, though, Netanyahu bade farewell to the negotiations with barely concealed relish. As a *Guardian* editorial of 28 April put it, 'The much-discussed pregnancy did not end in the birth of a peace agreement, or even an agreement to continue talking. The Palestinians describe it as having been nothing but a false pregnancy.' One veteran observer of the conflict, Henry Siegman, argued:

> Kerry should have known that the U.S. has no role in achieving an Israel–Palestinian peace if it is not prepared to use the leverage it possesses to get Israelis to abide by previous agreements and international law. Of course, there are domestic costs for any U.S. government that decides to get serious about demanding Israel to end its occupation. But there is something fatuous about our preaching to Israelis and Palestinians about the painful sacrifices they need to make to end this conflict when we refuse to do our far less painful part unless it is cost-free ...
>
> With the U.S. having failed to use its leverage over Israel, the only way to convince Israelis to accept a two-state outcome is a Palestinian non-violent, anti-apartheid struggle.[11]

Peter Beinart, the American writer and former editor of the *New Republic*, went further:

Reading the press, you'd think the Obama administration's effort to broker Israeli–Palestinian peace failed last week. That's not true. It failed three years ago.

In May 2011, eager to derail Mahmoud Abbas' bid for statehood at the UN, U.S. President Barack Obama laid out principles he hoped would kick-start Israeli–Palestinian talks. He said a Palestinian state 'should be based on the 1967 lines with mutually agreed swaps' and called for 'the full and phased withdrawal of Israeli military forces' as Palestinians took 'security responsibility in a sovereign, non-militarized state.'

Abbas described Obama's principles as 'a foundation with which we can deal positively.' Benjamin Netanyahu, by contrast, spiked them in Obama's face. As Obama sat beside him, chin in hand, Netanyahu both distorted and rebuffed, declaring that Israel 'cannot go back to the 1967 lines' – no mention of land swaps – 'because these lines are indefensible ... and we're going to have to have a long-term military presence along the Jordan [River].' Obama, a White House official later told me, 'felt the office of the presidency, the dignity of the office was insulted.'[12]

After the negotiations collapsed, John Kerry warned that if a two-state solution wasn't agreed upon soon, Israel would, in his words, risk becoming 'an apartheid state'.[13]

Naftali Bennett, Israel's Minister of the Economy and Habayit Hayehudi chairman, was not perturbed. He could not conceal his joy at the talks' failure, which he claimed he was instrumental in bringing about. He announced that 'the peace process was suicide', boasting, 'We saved the country.'[14]

Prime Minister Netanyahu assured the settlers that he was with them. Whether he said this as a politician or out of true conviction does not matter, because as a politician it made sense to align himself with the most powerful side – and the settlers were now the dominant political power in Israel. In so doing, his politics and ideological conviction have converged.

❧

In 1992, less than a year after the right-wing government of Yitzhak Shamir, under strong US pressure, had agreed to attend the international peace conference in Madrid, Shamir's government fell. On 13 July 1992, a coalition of the Labour Party with Meretz and Shas, supported but not joined by Hadash and the Arab Democratic Party, formed a new government. Led by Yitzhak Rabin, it proceeded with the negotiations that concluded with the signing of the Oslo Accords.

Perhaps, through his efforts, John Kerry had shown how impossible it is to persuade a right-wing Israeli government to be flexible and come to an agreement with its Palestinian neighbours. An optimistic assessment of the situation might even conclude that Kerry had driven home the point to the Israeli public, as well as to countries concerned about the Middle East conflict, that, in order to achieve peace, new elections were required, after which, hopefully, a government ready to make concessions for peace would emerge.

However, as it turned out, this was not to be. Rather

than fall after the failure of his government to make peace, Netanyahu, who has often been called a magician, found a way to save his coalition. And, as on numerous past occasions, this was done by waging yet another war against the Palestinians, in both the West Bank and the Gaza Strip.

6

SPRING 2014

Time and the bell have buried the day,
The black cloud carries the sun away ...

T. S. Eliot, Burnt Norton

The spring of 2014 was glorious. There had been plenty of rain and the hills and valleys were green and full of wild flowers. Migrating birds flew overhead on their long journey from Africa to Europe. The whole of historic Palestine and the Syrian Golan Heights were open and available for Israelis to hike in and enjoy. Meanwhile, 4.29 million Palestinians were confined behind walls and by closure orders, with 1.64 million in the Gaza Strip under siege for the past seven years and 2.65 million in the West Bank subject to a two-day closure order. This began on 12 April, the first day of Chol Hamo'ed, the intermediate period of the Passover holiday. On that day over 300,000 Israelis packed the country's forests, national parks (including Canada Park in the West Bank, built on the ruins of the three Palestinian villages destroyed immediately after the 1967 war) and nature reserves in Israel and the Golan Heights, including those around the Dead Sea in Israel and the West Bank, with another 50,000 crowding on to the beaches of Lake Tiberias.

Both sides of the lake are in Israeli hands. As the West Bank Palestinians were confined in what amounts to Bantustans, beyond which they cannot expand, Israel was enjoying the peace. The last forty years have been its most peaceful era. In that time it has not once been attacked by the military forces of a neighbouring Arab nation, or even threatened. It decides when and who it wants to attack and does so with impunity. Its economy is flourishing; unemployment is low, far lower than that in most European countries. It benefits from the occupation and is accepted in the world despite its record of breaking international law. It is a nation that has convinced itself – and in this it has been humoured by the world – it can perform miracles and get away with practically any legal contravention, large or small.

When Israelis look around, they see that all their enemies are weakened and defeated. The situation in Syria and Iraq is desperate, and things are not much better in Egypt. The Palestinians are reduced to begging, with their economy heavily dependent on the largesse of the EU and the US. Why should Israel want change? And why should it seek any sort of rapprochement with its neighbours? What incentive does it have to engage in peace talks when Israelis already have peace? It's true that the US and EU have been warning that there is the likelihood of a boycott looming, but how many countries base their current politics on what might be in store for them in the future?

With the failure of the US-sponsored negotiations, the popularity of the Right only rose. To the Israeli public, it appeared that, in refusing to be flexible, the Right had proved its worth, with policies that have brought peace and prosperity. Israeli leaders had arranged everything so well: the colonisation of the West Bank was proceeding at pace, while Gaza was kept under siege.

On 6 May 2014, Israelis were due to celebrate Independence Day for the sixty-sixth time. The evening before, spectacular fireworks shot into the night sky. Just in case any Palestinian community might have failed to appreciate Israel's hegemony over their land, Jewish settlements near Palestinian cities and villages had been given special subsidies to buy fireworks. As the magnificent displays burst overhead in nearby Psagot to the east, Dolev to the north and Beit El to the north-east, we the residents of Ramallah watched in anger.

After Israel's victory in the June War of 1967, Moshe Dayan, the Minister of Defence, had declared that Israel was now an empire. Why should this empire, which has become the sixth largest exporter of weapons in the world, submit to international law? They will continue on their triumphal path until, as a German aphorism succinctly puts it, they triumph themselves to death. Yet while actions against the Palestinians are not penalised, and indeed are supported by their many advocates throughout the world, that moment might take a long time in coming and much suffering will be caused in the interim.

So, as the Jewish citizens of Israel enjoyed the glorious spring, for their Palestinian neighbours the reality was very different. It wasn't just an issue of restrictions on movement, we were subject to frequent aggression on the part of the settlers and the army was more trigger-happy than ever.

The utter absurdity of the Palestinian situation was exemplified by an incident captured on video that took place on 8 February 2014 in Hebron. A Jewish settler living in the heart of the Arab Old City who, judging from his accent, seems to have been American, took umbrage at the sight of a Palestinian flag flying from the roof of an Arab house. He decided to take it down, so found a ladder and climbed up to the roof. But Israeli soldiers had placed barbed wire on the roof for the settlers' protection, so the man got caught in the wire. Tangled up, afraid and breathing heavily, he berated the Arab owner of the house, Shadi Sidar, saying, 'Why are you on my roof? Why are you on my roof?'

Shadi replied, 'Why are you coming to my roof? Would I be welcome in your house?'

The settler said, 'I live in Israel. This is Eretz Israel. It is all mine. Why do you fly the flag?'

'This is Hebron, not Israel. I'm not in Tel Aviv. This is Palestine.'

'What is Palestine? All this is Eretz Israel,' the settler declared, adding, 'It is mine, all mine.'

At this point an Israeli soldier came to the settler's rescue. He told Shadi that flying a flag from his house is forbidden, which is not true. The soldier could see that Israeli flags were flying from the roofs of all the houses inhabited by Israeli settlers. After threatening to arrest Shadi because he had dared to raise the flag, the soldier eventually succeeded in having him remove it.[1]

This was but one of many incidents that took place every day in Hebron and other parts of the West Bank where Israeli settlers live alongside Palestinian Arabs as hostile neighbours. Other depressing incidents were also taking place elsewhere in the West Bank.

Seventeen-year-old Nadim Nuwara attends St George Secondary School, which was established by the Greek Orthodox Church and is next to my house. On 15 May 2014, when Palestinians commemorate the Nakba, he was demonstrating against the Israeli practice of administrative detention near the Israeli military prison of Ofra in Betunia, close to Ramallah. The detainees had gone on hunger strike on 24 April, demanding to know the charges for which they had been incarcerated. This type of detention is implemented solely on the basis of an administrative order, without either indictment or trial. As of 23 June 2014, there were 200 Palestinians under administrative detention, eighty of whom were participating in the hunger strike. The detention order can be renewed repeatedly, so that the detainee does not know the length of time he or she is to be held. Over the years, thousands of Palestinians have been kept in Israeli custody as administrative detainees for extended periods of time.[2]

That day in May, Israeli soldiers fired live ammunition at Nadim Nuwara and his sixteen-year-old friend Mohammad Abu Thaher, killing them both. Three others were also wounded. The army denied that it had shot the bullet that killed Nadim, despite the video showing this (they claimed that the film was edited). Later an autopsy proved that he was killed by an Israeli bullet. Sarah Whitson, Middle East and North Africa director of Human Rights Watch, said after the shooting, 'The wilful killing of civilians by Israeli security forces as part of the occupation is a war crime.' On 12 November 2014, Israel finally admitted that the gun had been fired by an Israeli soldier, who was subsequently arrested.

Nadim had been considered by his family a fortunate young man, for he had experienced several near misses with death. He was born prematurely, when his mother was in her seventh month. He contracted jaundice when he finally left hospital. As a young boy he was hit by a car and thrown up in the air, but survived. Yet he wasn't fortunate enough to survive the occupation. He was shot by an Israeli soldier who, as two *Haaretz* journalists reported, had fired 'apparently because of "boredom"'.[3]

᪲

US Middle East Special Envoy Martin Indyk said that for him the most poignant moment during the nine-month negotiations came when the two sides failed to agree on even a framework to extend negotiations. Majid Faraj, the Palestinian director of intelligence, turned to the Israelis across the table and said, 'You just don't see us.'[4]

He could have said the same of the Americans, who throughout the process had not thought to negotiate with the Palestinians and had never presented them with any written draft of the proposed agreement which they expected the Palestinians to accept with gratitude.[5]

If the American superpower can afford not to see the Palestinian, the Israelis cannot. But is it any wonder that the Israelis don't see us when Israel has orchestrated a life of separation between the two nations, with different roads for each, a wall separating the two sides and warning signs on roads leading to Palestinian cities and villages lest Israelis wander in by mistake? And when Israel has changed the law to make it possible for Israelis to settle in most parts of the territory and violate the rights of Palestinians to property and personal protection with impunity, while expecting the Palestinians security forces to cooperate with them in restraining Palestinians from attacking Israeli forces or Jewish settlers?

But everything was about to change. Soon after the talks ended, President Abbas took a strategic decision to sign a reconciliation deal between Fatah and Hamas whereby a Palestinian unity government was formed to run the West Bank and the Gaza Strip. This largely came about because both sides, for different reasons, were desperate. Hamas had no money to pay the salaries of its 43,000 employees in Gaza. The change of government in Egypt had brought in a regime that despised Hamas, which they regarded as a branch of the Muslim Brotherhood. Along with this, the limitations imposed on the Rafah crossing almost completely blocked traffic in the tunnels, depriving Hamas of the taxes they collected on smuggled goods coming in from Sinai to Gaza. Gaza residents found themselves in an increasing economic stranglehold.

Given this crisis, Hamas was forced to sign the reconciliation agreement with the Palestinian Authority in the hope that the PA would supply the funding it needed. But that hope proved false, because of the banking limits that the US imposed, spurred on by Israel, that prevented the transfer of funds from Qatar to Gaza. At the same time, Hamas was continuing to pursue the military option, which was by then looking more promising.

As for the Palestinian Authority, their strategy of ending the occupation through negotiations with Israel had proved unsuccessful and was unpopular. It was despair, then, that brought the two together and led to the formation of a Palestinian unity government.

Had Benjamin Netanyahu been interested in reaching a peace agreement with the Palestinians, he would have welcomed this development, because it meant that any agreement made with Israel would involve all Palestinians, in both the West Bank and the Gaza Strip.

Instead he went on the offensive, comparing Hamas to IS (Islamic State) and Al-Qaeda, and said that the 'critical thing' was for Abbas to break up the Palestinian unity government. Netanyahu assumed that linking Hamas and the jihadists in Iraq was the best way to taint the Palestinian organisation and portray it as an enemy of America, while casting Israel as the force that was confronting the extremists on America's behalf and possibly in its stead.

He declared, 'Hamas is like the Islamist movements that you see in Syria and in Iraq and elsewhere in the Middle East – it is committed to a savagery that not only includes the demise of the State of Israel, but actually the establishment of these Islamist realms – unforgiving violent realms – that oppose peace.'

He went on to tell the US that Israel was fighting Hamas 'Just as you're fighting Al-Qaida everywhere you can. I think that if you are trying to make peace you can't have a unity pact with Al-Qaida – in this case with Hamas.'[6]

So now the scope of terrorism, so far associated with the murderous group Al-Qaeda, has been expanded to include Hamas.

There was a time, not too long ago, when the Palestine Liberation Organisation was the enemy and Hamas was not even a proscribed organisation. The oft-repeated propaganda line then was that the PLO wanted to destroy Israel, so how could the country agree to recognise it and engage in peace talks with it? Now the PLO has renounced violence and its chairman, Mahmoud Abbas, has repeatedly confirmed that he believes negotiation is the only way to achieve peace, and yet Israel refuses to negotiate. It will have become clear by now that this stalemate is not because of Israel's adversaries or the positions they hold or what their charter states. Rather, peace has not been achieved because, as experience has repeatedly shown, Israel does not want it.

But not everything was going Israel's way. The Israeli government came in for considerable international disapproval for allowing the talks to fail. In addition, the EU and the US did not boycott the unity government, as Israel wanted. And there was internal pressure as well. The prime minister was strongly criticised for releasing so many Palestinian prisoners in the Gilad Shalit prisoner-exchange deal.[7] Whereas this had brought him popularity at the time and his ratings in October 2011 rose, now that one of the freed men was suspected of murdering an Israeli Jew, Netanyahu's fortunes changed. Those in the government who were against further prisoner-exchange deals began pressing for legislation that would prohibit future deals and the law was passed on 3 November 2014. This was another way of saying that they did not want negotiations with the Palestinians to continue. As we saw earlier, these had come to a halt after the government refused to release the last batch of prisoners, despite promises made when negotiations began.

The line of the Netanyahu government was now that Abbas could not, as he claimed, be someone who wanted to make peace with Israel as he had joined with Hamas. He would have to choose between peace with Israel and unity with Hamas. This, of course, was just empty rhetoric, because Israel was not offering Abbas an acceptable solution for ending the conflict. The preference of the Israeli government under Netanyahu's leadership was to act tough with the Palestinians and pursue their war on so-called 'terror'. In the process, the Palestinians would continue to be denied the opportunity to lead normal lives.

Any hopes for a negotiated peace that had been nurtured during the previous nine months came to an end soon after the collapse of the negotiations when, on the evening of 12 June, three Israelis studying at a Jewish settlement were kidnapped.

Israel responded by launching the biblical-sounding 'Operation Brother's Keeper'. This was a large-scale crackdown on what it called Hamas's terrorist infrastructure and personnel in the West Bank. Ostensibly it was aimed at securing the release of the kidnapped teenagers. It involved deploying thousands of soldiers in the Hebron area and beyond, house-to-house searches and hunting through cellars and caves. What it managed to do was to create a routine of domination and intimidation as a form of collective punishment. In the course of this operation ten

Palestinians were killed in numerous raids, and between 350 and 600 Palestinians were arrested, including nearly all of Hamas's West Bank leadership. Among those arrested were many people who had only recently been freed under the terms of the Gilad Shalit prisoner exchange. This meant that Netanyahu could both atone for his earlier 'crime' of releasing Palestinian prisoners, which the Right held against him, and show his mettle.

The search for the abducted Israelis continued on the assumption that the young men were still alive. It later transpired that soon after the abduction took place, the Israeli government, the security forces and the police were aware – from a recording the police managed to get of a telephone conversation one of the abductors made – that the three kidnapped youths were killed straight away. And yet the authorities chose to keep this information from the public, declaring, 'Our working assumption is that the three are alive.'

By hiding this vital information from the public, they sought to cultivate worldwide interest and sympathy in the kidnapping. In this way it became easier to justify the barbaric and brutal retaliatory action the security forces and army were taking against the civilian population in the West Bank, especially but not exclusively in the south, where the abduction took place.

On the morning of 18 June 2014, my wife and I woke up and saw on the television news the President of the Board of Trustees of Birzeit University, Dr Hanna Nasser, speaking to journalists during the early hours of the morning from the besieged campus of the university, with Israeli soldiers and jeeps in the background. Among them was one woman wearing her hair in a ponytail and carrying a notebook. The army had arrived after midnight, crashed through the gate, captured the guards, taken their keys and mobile phones, imprisoned them in one room and proceeded to go through the campus, searching and confiscating material, which they put on a pickup truck. So far during the occupation, the army had refrained from entering the university campus; now they forced their way not only into Birzeit University but also into most of the other West Bank universities as well.

What followed seemed like a protracted version of the 2002 invasion of the West Bank. Now as then, the victims of the operation included many innocent and vulnerable civilians. It also threatened the security cooperation between the Israeli and Palestinian forces that had been proceeding very well for a decade. For the first time, the Israeli Army entered the Palestinian cities of Ramallah and Nablus, which the Oslo Accords stated were in Area A and so under full Palestinian territorial jurisdiction, without informing or coordinating with the Palestinian security forces.

Without providing any evidence linking the teenagers' abduction to Hamas, Netanyahu blamed the Islamic faction and started to make daily revenge attacks on the Palestinian population under occupation. Although the kidnapping took place in the south of the West Bank, the searches, arrests and destruction of property were not confined exclusively to either members of Hamas or to the south of the West Bank. So perfect for Netanyahu's purposes was the timing that many in the occupied territories believed that the whole affair had been choreographed by Mossad. Could it be just another of those fabrications by the Israeli authorities to further their plans against the Palestinians, justify the harsh actions they were taking, even though they had planned everything beforehand, as they often did, and gain a high level of sympathy throughout the world? It is not unusual for this political struggle to be acted out as a stage drama in which the most important consideration is which protagonist can win the sympathies of the audience. It was a perfect case of reading history backwards to confirm a conspiracy theory.

It is not that the Israeli Army should not search for missing people. But abductions happen all over the world and entire civilian populations are not held hostage, prevented from going on with their lives until those missing are found. Yet the people of Israel have so internalised their colonial status that they feel they can decide whether or not we Palestinians, the civilian society under their rule, are allowed to lead normal lives. When Galim Shaar, the mother of one of the kidnapped teenagers, addressed the Knesset, she said, 'At a time when the Jewish people live fearfully in their land, the Palestinian people go about their routine ...'[8]

The government made no attempt to conceal their broader objectives, which went beyond searching for the three abductees. 'Even if we locate and rescue the kidnapped boys, we won't cease this operation until we feel we have exhausted it,' Defence Minister Moshe Ya'alon declared. 'The operation must continue as long as it continues,' Israel Defence Forces Chief of Staff, Benny Gantz, said. He went on to explain that while the operation's main goal was to find the boys and their abductors, the 'ancillary goal' was to cause more damage to Hamas.[9]

As *Haaretz* reported on 23 June 2014:

> If the goal is to cause more damage to Hamas, on the assumption – as yet unproven – that Hamas perpetrated the kidnapping, it's legitimate to ask why the Shin Bet security service wasn't taking action against Hamas operatives even before the abduction. The purpose of rounding up 'the usual suspects' is similarly unclear. If the goal is to cause the Fatah–Hamas reconciliation and unity government to break up, policy makers must explain how this goal will aid in finding the kidnapped teens and their abductors. And even if we assume this is a worthy goal in its own right, how will searching houses, clashing with innocent civilians and killing demonstrators help persuade the Palestinian Authority to break with Hamas?[10]

During all this time we were bombarded with images of the three missing boys. Israeli demonstrators marched down the streets of West Jerusalem, chanting slogans such as 'Death to Arabs' and 'A Jew is a brother, an Arab is a bastard', intending to beat up any Arabs they came across. But as we have already seen, it is often difficult to distinguish between a Jew and an Arab by appearance, so they had to ask passers-by for the time in order to find out from their accent who was Jewish and who wasn't.

I had heard these chants long before in the streets of Jerusalem. This is how I began my book *The Sealed Room* (1992), quoting from my diary for 3 September 1990:

> I was watching the news on Israeli television, reporting

the aftermath of the stabbing to death of two Israelis by a Palestinian.

A large angry crowd had gathered on the highway leading from Jerusalem to the West Bank town of Bethlehem. An Israeli driving by stopped and told the camera, 'They must go.' He spoke with unmistakable conviction, referring to us, the Palestinians. Before he drove on, he added, 'There is no other way.'

They came to our country, occupied it and now they say 'the Palestinians must go' as though it were the most natural and necessary thing in the world.

The Israeli police stood by, listening. They watched as the mob expressed itself, not only in words but also by stoning all passing cars with blue licence plates marking them as belonging to West Bank Palestinians. An Israeli soldier was suddenly stirred. Perhaps by his unexpected discovery that he agreed with the sentiment being expressed. He grabbed a Palestinian youth from behind and kicked him. The Palestinian turned and with visible rage called the soldier '*Maniak!*' [Bugger]

The camera now moved on to show us the rest of the rowdy crowd chanting, '*Mavit le Aravim! Mavit le Aravim!*' [Death to the Arabs]

We watched, and I thought of the horrors to come.

A quarter of a century later I was witnessing the results of years of mounting fanaticism and the promotion of the settlement enterprise. Now, rather than kick youths in the backside, Israeli soldiers shoot them dead. But worse was yet to come.

On 30 June search teams found the bodies of the three missing teenagers near Hebron. Two days later sixteen-year-old Mohammed Abu Khdeir was murdered in a display of brutality the likes of which we had never experienced before.

Mohammed was kidnapped by Israeli Jews near his home in East Jerusalem. Three of the gang, all apparently young, have confessed to taking him to the Jerusalem Forest, stabbing him a number of times and then burning him alive.

According to the anthropologist Tamir Lion, who is head of research at the Ethos Institute, 'Today I can say, and everyone who works with youth will say it, Jewish youth in Israel hate Arabs without connection to their parents or their own party affiliation and their own political opinions.' He thinks the reason is a deep uncertainty about Israel's direction: 'The state of Israel in recent years is looking for its ethos, that is to say, "Where are we going?"' Without clear answers, 'You always withdraw to the most primitive ethos: us and them. It becomes a group that defines itself not as what it is, but what it hates.'[11]

Jewish settler violence is obviously nothing new in the West Bank. It has been going on since the early 1980s. My colleagues and I at Al-Haq documented the settlers' violations and published our findings. We also cooperated with Israeli civil rights activists to have them investigated by the Israeli law enforcement authorities. These efforts resulted in a report by the deputy of the Israeli attorney general, Yehudit Karp. The report, which took a number of years to prepare and publish, found 'serious shortcomings' in investigations when Palestinians were victims. It criticised the police for failing to investigate charges seriously, noted delays in pursuing cases and found fault with the separation between regular and military police. The report advised a reassessment of the instructions given to Israeli soldiers for opening fire on civilians, recommended an increase in the number of civilian police in the West Bank, and criticised the refusal of Jewish witnesses – especially settlers in the West Bank – to cooperate with police in investigations relating to Palestinian victims. Karp resigned after the Likud-led government neglected the report's findings.[12]

It is not that gruesome acts of murder have not happened before in our cruel part of the world and were not documented. Yet this latest murder, which involved burning a Palestinian alive, was not like any other. As I wrote at the time, it was intended to communicate a message that goes something like this:

> We, Israeli Jews, have the right to a full life and enjoyment of this land which we call Greater Israel. And you, Palestinian Arabs, have no place here. You cannot have your fruit trees be safe from uprooting, or your crops from destruction, or your private property from unlawful seizure, or your hikes in the hills in safety, or your visit to the spring next to your village, or your drive to the sea, or your reunification with members of your family and friends forced to live away even if their homes are only a few miles away because you don't belong here. This land is ours. It is not yours. And if after all this you still do not get it then we will take your children to the forest and this time we will not only shoot or stab them to death but we'll burn

them alive so that their bodies get charred and in this way we'll purify our land from your odious presence. Perhaps then you might finally get the message we've been trying to pass to you all those years.[13]

It was as though, with this horrific murder, the Palestinians had had enough. The situation was reminiscent of the first Intifada, which was ignited at the end of 1987 by the killing of Palestinian workers by an extremist as they waited for transport to take them back to their homes in the West Bank. This time, the shock caused by reports of the charred and mutilated body of Abu Khdeir was the tipping point and started a series of actions by youths in East Jerusalem the likes of which the city had not seen for many years. Immediately the resistance spread to other parts of the West Bank. Had it not been for the efforts of the Palestinian security forces a third Intifada would have started. The hand of Mahmoud Abbas, who always said the second Intifada was a mistake, came down heavily, making sure another round would not start.

No longer were Palestinian communities in different parts of the occupied territories prepared to remain without protection or depend on getting it from the Palestinian security forces. First in Bil'in, then in Hebron, communal protection committees were established and other areas soon followed suit. Perhaps with popular resistance to its aggressive brutal ways, Israel would begin to notice the Palestinians under its rule. But these efforts were not to last.

❧

In some ways what happened in June 2014 could be explained by feelings of political insecurity on the part of the coalition government headed by Benjamin Netanyahu. That the US-sponsored peace negotiations collapsed on the issue of the release of prisoners was a telling point, highlighting the differences between Abbas and Netanyahu. While Abbas genuinely wanted the conflict to end with a peace agreement with Israel, Netanyahu wanted to perpetuate it. Abbas wanted to turn a new page with the negotiations, but Netanyahu would not let him. The present government is attached to the old ways, to fighting what it calls terror, and promotes the sale of weapons and weapons systems it produces to fight this threat. To promote peace would thus require painful and costly adjustments and cause the loss of very lucrative opportunities that are defended by strong lobbies in Israel. There is no evidence that the country is prepared to make the change.

Haaretz columnist Chemi Shalev draws worrying conclusions from recent events:

> But make no mistake: the gangs of Jewish ruffians manhunting for Arabs are no aberration. Theirs was not a one-time outpouring of uncontrollable rage following the discovery of the bodies of the three kidnapped students. Their inflamed hatred does not exist in a vacuum: it is an ongoing presence, growing by the day, encompassing ever larger segments of Israeli society, nurtured in a public environment of resentment, insularity and victimhood, fostered and fed by politicians

and pundits – some cynical, some sincere – who have grown weary of democracy and its foibles and who long for an Israel, not to put too fine a point on it, of one state, one nation and, somewhere down the line, one leader.[14]

For those like me who live under occupation, it was equally disquieting to read Chris Hedges on the Truthdig website reminding us of Raul Hilberg's work, 'Destruction of the European Jews', in which 'he chronicled a process of repression that at first was "relatively mild" but led, step by step, to the Holocaust. It started with legal discrimination and ended with mass murder. "The destructive process was a development that was begun with caution and ended without restraint," Hilberg wrote.'[15]

After missile attacks by both Hamas and Israel, on the night of 6 July an Israeli missile was fired at the house of an alleged Hamas operative in Khan Yunis, killing seven people. The following day, Hamas referred to the incident as a 'massacre against women and children [and] a horrendous war crime' and claimed 'all Israelis have now become legitimate targets'; it then assumed formal responsibility for launching rocket attacks on Israel in increasing numbers. By 7 July Hamas had fired 100 rockets from Gaza at Israeli territory; at the same time, the Israeli Air Force bombed several sites in Gaza. Early on 8 July the IAF bombed fifty targets in the Gaza Strip. Israel's military also stopped a militant infiltration from the sea. Brigadier General Moti Almoz, the chief spokesman of the Israeli military, said, 'We have been instructed by the political echelon to hit Hamas hard.' As conditions for a ceasefire,

Hamas insisted that Israel end all attacks on Gaza, release those rearrested during the crackdown in the West Bank, lift the blockade on Gaza and return to the ceasefire conditions of 2012. Thus began a vicious and destructive fifty-day attack by Israel on the Gaza Strip and the firing of thousands of missiles by Hamas on Israel.

If the events that took place in June had shocked me as never before, we were now facing an even greater shock: the pounding of the Gaza Strip from air, sea and land. All hopes for a language of peace had ended and we began to hear once again the language of war, with all its false allure.

7

WAR ON GAZA

I am the enemy you killed, my friend.

Wilfred Owen, 'Strange Meeting'

The latest aggression against the Gaza Strip was the third
and deadliest war between Israel and Hamas in six years.
When it started, I was already reeling from the collapse of
the US-sponsored peace talks and at having to add John
Kerry's name to the long list of people who had, over the
years, tried and failed to bring an end to conflict in the
Middle East. The brutal murder of Mohammed Abu Khdeir
had only added to my depression.

No less distressing was the futility of the response of
the young Palestinians in the streets of East Jerusalem,
who felt compelled to act. The father of one of the boys
who were arrested had told his son to remain indoors, but

the boy said, 'I'm afraid they'll burn me like they burned Abu Khdeir, so I won't stay at home.'[1] Children as young as thirteen ended up rioting in the streets. They would cover their faces with keffiyehs and brandish slingshots in poses that photograph well but only result in more fallen youths with terrible, sometimes fatal wounds.

My own weapons of struggle had proved no more effective. All my attempts over many years at invoking the law, municipal and international, had come to nothing. This was confirmed when, during the war on Gaza, I reluctantly turned on the television and watched the Al Jazeera English-language programme *Head to Head*. When the former settler leader Dani Dayan was challenged and reminded that he was living on stolen Palestinian land and that the Jewish settlements he had helped to establish were in violation of international law, he simply shrugged, as if to say, 'I'm here to stay. Move me out if you have the power.' We obviously don't, and it wasn't clear to me what anyone could do to force Israel to withdraw from the Palestinian territories and make it possible for us to establish our state.

On the eve of the Israeli assault on Gaza it felt as though we Palestinians had come to the end of the road, having exhausted all the different means of resistance we had attempted over four and a half decades in the course of pursuing our liberation. We had to either learn to live with discrimination and diminished rights, or leave.

Meanwhile, Hamas declared that if Israel dared to send its army to attack Gaza the gates of hell would open wide and they would face resistance the likes of which they had never previously encountered. But I had my doubts. Over the years, we have heard so many promises from Arab and Palestinian leaders who said they were ready for a real fight against Israel, acquired stocks of weapons and received training from as far afield as Vietnam, but their promises came to nothing. It was difficult for me to believe that this time it would be any different and an Israeli attack would be met with resistance so strong that it would cause our enemy to sober up and seek other ways to resolve the conflict than by destroying the Palestinian side. Perhaps in my case the psychological warfare Israel waged had been successful.

As it turned out, when the assault began it became clear that militarily Hamas and Islamic Jihad, a smaller militant organisation, were well prepared. They had dug extensive tunnels, they had planned attacks against Israel from the sea and they had amassed a large arsenal of missiles, both home-made and imported from other conflict areas in the region. By the end of fifty days of fighting, Hamas and Islamic Jihad had fired 4,564 rockets and mortars from Gaza into Israel, killing sixty-six Israeli soldiers, five civilians (two of them unprotected Bedouins) and one Thai worker, wounding 450 soldiers and eighty civilians, and causing massive economic loss. Watching all this, I wondered how many bombs would have to strike Israel, how many soldiers and civilians would have to die, how much economic loss the country would have to suffer before it woke up and came to the conclusion that only through negotiations could peace be achieved.

As the conflict proceeded a poll published by the Israel Democracy Institute found 92 per cent of Jewish Israelis believed the war was justified and almost half thought appropriate force had been used by the Israeli military. Only a few courageous voices expressed outrage at what Israel was doing to the civilian population in the Gaza Strip and at the cynical manner in which Israeli generals described their periodic incursions into Gaza using the dehumanising term 'mowing the lawn'. A handful of analysts pointed out that the assault would not result in greater security for Israel.

No less hardened were the hearts of people in the West Bank, who had no compassion left for the Israelis who were bombarded with thousands of missiles, however ramshackle and unaimed. They had been put through too much suffering themselves over too many years.

I experienced increasing outrage at what was taking place so close to home. Feelings of deep and intense anger, long suppressed, began to come to the surface. My life has been embittered by the Israeli state, starting from when its fighters expelled my parents from their home in Jaffa and extending to the more recent destruction of the landscape that I cherish so much, with all the concomitant suffering in between.

How, I wondered, have such hardened warriors emerged from among our defeated ranks? I remembered visiting Gaza in 2000 (the last occasion I was allowed to enter the Strip), when I was the legal adviser for a newly built power plant there that had been knocked out of action early on in the war when a fuel depot was hit, leaving over a million people in Gaza without electricity. Movement between the West Bank and Gaza was restricted and, after being delayed on the Israeli border for several hours, I was picked up on the Gaza side by a young man in a van who seemed close to

Hamas and was obviously enamoured of its tactics. On the way he told me how, when he used to be active with other Palestinian factions operating in the Gaza Strip, the Israeli military would always do enough to stop them before they managed to leave their homes. Things were entirely different once he became engaged with Hamas. Secrecy was observed and Hamas has been more successful in its military operations against Israel than any Palestinian faction had been in the past, he said.

As the assault proceeded, I was mesmerised by the impressive tactics of defence and attack of these fellow Palestinians whose lives had taken such a different trajectory from my own and who followed beliefs and shared a world-view so different from mine.

During the first Intifada, from 1987 to 1991, statements made under oath were collected by Al-Haq fieldworkers in Gaza concerning attacks by Israeli soldiers against Gazan men living in refugee camps (about half of Gazans are refugees). They spoke of how the Israeli soldiers forced their way into the crowded homes of Palestinians and proceeded to insult and beat fathers in front of their children. I remember wondering then how those children would grow up and what would become of them. Gazans also endured humiliation as they crossed the border with Israel to seek work or medical treatment, in addition to years of poverty and lack of employment opportunities. Dr Eyad El-Sarraj, the late, much-loved psychiatrist from Gaza, put it well when he said:

> During the first intifada, studies showed that 55 percent
> of the children had witnessed their fathers being

humiliated or beaten by Israeli soldiers. The psychological impact of this is stunning. The father, normally the authority figure, comes to be seen as somebody who is helpless, who can't even protect himself – let alone his children. So children became more militant, more violent. People are the products of their environment. Children who have seen so much inhumanity – basically the Israeli occupation policies – inevitably come out with inhuman responses. That's really how to understand the suicide bombings.[2]

Was it any wonder, then, after so much violence committed by Israel against the population of the Gaza Strip during and since the first Intifada, that such conditions would give rise to a committed group of determined and hardened fighters who would be willing to put their all into the struggle in their determination to either live with dignity or die?

Addressing her fellow Israelis, Amira Hass wrote: 'Those who turned Gaza into an internment and punishment camp for 1.8 million human beings should not be surprised that they tunnel underneath the earth. Those who sow strangling, siege and isolation reap rocket fire.' And she ended by proposing: 'You want to prevent escalation? Now is the time: Open up the Gaza Strip, let the people return to the world, the West Bank, and to their families and families in Israel. Let them breathe, and they will find out that life is more beautiful than death.'[3]

Judging from the graffiti that Israeli soldiers left in homes they had occupied during the assault, they did not share the sentiment. When Ahmed Owedat returned to his home in Burij eighteen days after Israeli soldiers took it over in the middle of the night, he found the words 'Burn Gaza down' and 'Good Arab = dead Arab' scratched into his coffee table.[4]

Such vicious statements were similar to ones left by Israeli soldiers in Palestinian homes they took over in Ramallah during the invasion of the city in 2002, in the operation Israel called 'Defensive Shield'. Then the only real resistance was in Jenin. One of the Palestinian heroes of that battle was Ala el-Sabagr, of the Al-Aqsa Brigade, a militant offshoot of Fatah.

In the 2004 Dutch–Israeli documentary film *Arna's Children* there is an image I will never forget. It shows the young Ala sitting in the ruins of his home, which has been blown up by the Israeli Army, his round face full of repressed anger. That film, directed by the late Juliano Mer Khamis and Danniel Danniel, is about a children's theatre group in Jenin established by Juliano's mother. It followed the life of Ala and his colleagues from when they were children to the time they became courageous fighters. It came as a revelation to me, helping me to understand how other people's experiences – so different from my own – took them down the path of militant reaction to the Israeli occupation. Ala continued to fight until he was killed. As I watched 50,000 heroic Hamas fighters standing up to the strongest army in the Middle East, as no other Arab army has done since 1973, I remembered *Arna's Children*.

In the course of the fifty days of fighting Israel dropped 20,000 tons of explosives on an area of 360 square kilometres.[5] Idan Barir, an Israeli artillery captain compared the use of artillery to Russian roulette:

Artillery fire ... is the absolute opposite of precise sniper fire ... [it] is nothing but a large fragmentation grenade which is meant to kill everyone within a 60-meter radius ... they are not meant to hit specific targets ... since the launch of Operation Protective Edge, the IDF has already shot thousands of artillery shells at different parts of the Gaza Strip. The shells have caused unbearable damage to human life and tremendous destruction to infrastructure ...[6]

The severity and barbarity of the war waged by Israel against Gaza could not be concealed despite slippery public relations on the part of the Israeli Army, which was keen to be seen as playing fair by giving warnings to civilians, even though they had no place to go; nor could such attempts stop Israel from being seen to contravene international law. The army's efforts included the macabre 'knock on the roof' warnings to alert residents before dropping bombs on their houses. In an attempt to avoid recrimination for causing such large numbers of civilian deaths, Israeli Defence Forces were reported to have used recorded telephone messages to warn more than 100,000 residents in two Gaza City neighbourhoods to evacuate their homes. This blanket warning was then followed by a call to occupants telling them they have five minutes to get out.[7] As Al Jazeera has shown, however, the army does not wait five minutes but fires the missiles earlier, even though five minutes is not long enough for an entire family, especially one with young children, to leave the house.

In true Orwellian fashion, the Gaza assault and the

reporting of events were replete with enough misleading terms to give a discourse analyst years of explication. The propaganda battle began with the official Hebrew name Israel gave its attack on Gaza, which translates as 'resolute cliff'. As Steven Poole of the *Guardian* pointed out, this was meant 'to assure its victims of the futility of resistance. Only a fool would try to fight a cliff.' In English the name used was 'Operation Protective Edge'. As an Israeli military spokesman explained, this was chosen to 'give a more defensive connotation'. Poole added, 'The bombing was supposedly "protective", though not of those bombed.' Rarely was the fighting referred to by Israel as a 'war'; instead it was a 'clash' or a 'conflict'. Israeli fighters were referred to as 'soldiers', while Hamas were 'terrorists' who had built 'terror tunnels'. The Israeli prime minister, Benjamin Netanyahu, said that Hamas had turned UN facilities into 'terrorist hotspots'. To quote Poole again: 'A terrorist hotspot is rather like a Wi-Fi hotspot: when you are within range, you can be sure of getting a terrorist. Of course, if your means of getting him is a large bomb, you will certainly get a bunch of other people too.'[8]

Uri Avnery, the veteran Israeli writer and peace activist, has pointed out that it is as though two wars are being fought:

The Israeli media are now totally subservient. There is no independent reporting. 'Military correspondents' are not allowed into Gaza to see for themselves ... I escape from this brainwashing by listening to both sides, switching all the time between Israeli TV stations and Aljazeera (in Arabic and in English). What I see is

two different wars, happening at the same time on two
different planets ...

He then goes on to describe how Hamas is presented to
Israelis as the incarnation of evil. Their leaders are not
commanding from underground posts but are 'hiding'
there; they store weapons in mosques, schools and
hospitals; they use the civilian population as 'human
shields' and have dug 'terror tunnels'. He contrasts this
with how they are seen in Arab eyes as patriotic sons of the
suffering population who grew up in the house now being
destroyed.[9]

In an attempt to convey the suffering of the people
in Gaza, the Israeli human rights organisation B'Tselem
produced a radio advertisement which simply read out
the names of children killed in Gaza. The Israel Broadcast
Authority refused to air it. The organisation appealed to
the High Court, which refused the appeal.

Whatever the attempts, through language or manipu-
lation of the media, to change perceptions of the terrible
reality, the loss of life and extent of the destruction caused
in Gaza were horrific. Once again the Israeli military was
attempting and failing to 'etch the consciousness of the
Palestinians', as the then Chief of Staff, Moshe Ya'alon, put
it in 2002, in accordance with the cynical 'map of pain'
drawn up by the Israeli Army's General Staff.[10]

This attempt at 'etching' our consciousness was not
the first. As I reported in my book *Palestinian Walks* (2008),
Ariel Sharon had already tried 'to etch in the consciousness of the Palestinians a new geography' of Palestine. It
seems that, for all their etching, the Israelis keep failing.

The severe pain suffered by the people of Gaza did not cause them to turn against their leaders either, as Israel had hoped; but nor did the Hamas missiles fired at Israel make the country believe in negotiations rather than war, as I and other Palestinians had hoped. Even before the war was over the usual suspects were assuring the Israeli public that this would not be the last war, that it was only an interlude before the next, more destructive one.

The Israeli historian Benny Morris, echoing the views of others, wrote:

> What should we do next time? The answer is clear and well known. All that's needed is the courage to start down this path and the determination to finish the job. It won't be either easy or quick. We're talking about reoccupying the entire Gaza Strip and destroying Hamas as a military organization, and perhaps also as a political one (it's reasonable to think that destroying Hamas' army will badly weaken Hamas as a political movement).[11]

And then, to leave no doubt that any hope could emerge from this painful experience, the much-lauded man of peace and former Israeli president, Shimon Peres, who during his tenure as prime minister built more settlements than any other Israeli leader and was instrumental in arming Israel with nuclear weapons, said in an interview with the BBC: 'The extensive Hamas rocket fire from Gaza over the past month has made it difficult to justify withdrawing from the West Bank as part of a future peace deal with the Palestinians.' Then, repeating the same lie often used by Israeli propagandists to deny that Israel had placed Gaza under siege, he added:

> Look, we left Gaza willingly, unilaterally ... We handed over to the Palestinians a free, open Gaza. Which is a beautiful strip of a beautiful beach. They could have developed it for tourism, for fishing, for agriculture. We don't understand, frankly, why are they fighting? What are they shooting? What are the reasons? We left. What is the purpose? They want to be free? They are free.[12]

Not only had Israel placed the Gaza Strip under siege for seven years, but it prohibited the Palestinians from exploiting the large natural gas field off the coast of Gaza that was discovered in 2000 by British Gas. It is claimed that the Strip has natural gas reserves worth $4 billion which could have saved the Gaza economy.

To dispel any glimmer of hope left, even before the war had ended Gideon Levy, exercising to the full the pessimism of the intellect, wrote:

> We still haven't reached an agreement, yet that agreement is already behind us ... This is what the masses clamored for in the biggest protest during the war – for quiet for the south. Quiet. Simply quiet. Who could be for terror and against quiet? ... This must be Israelis' most self-righteous and revolting demand. They want quiet and the hell with the surrounding noise and its causes. Let Gaza suffocate and the West Bank ...[13]

The sanctification of the quiet reminded me of another time when, during the Gulf War, Israelis entered their 'sealed rooms', and wore their gas masks to avoid contamination by the presumed chemical missiles which Saddam Hussein was supposed to possess. This time they found safety under the protection of the Iron Dome defence system. At the end of the first Gulf War I wrote addressing the Israelis:

I want to leave my sealed room,
will you leave yours?
Then we'll meet halfway.
What do you say?[14]

This time I didn't even bother.

At the end of fifty days of intense and destructive fighting, a ceasefire was agreed. Others have documented the immense losses of Palestinian life, homes and infrastructure. Suffice it to say here that the war left 2,131 dead, of whom 501 were children, and 450,000 people unable to access municipal water due to damage and/or low pressure.[15] Estimates suggest that it will take seven years to repair the physical damage. The emotional and psychological damage caused to civilians might never be recovered from.

Six weeks after the assault on Gaza ended, the Palestinian reconciliation government of Hamas and Fatah held their first ministerial meeting in Gaza. The government's convoy travelled from Ramallah, passing through Israeli territory. This was obviously with the permission of Israel, headed by the same prime minister, Benjamin Netanyahu, who only three months earlier had done all he could to stop the payments to its officials in Gaza, who had refused to recognise its legitimacy, boycotted its ministers, denounced it worldwide and told his public that it was a government of terror. It was this wages crisis and the resulting economic crisis, as well as Israel's determination to prevent reconciliation, that had precipitated the war on Gaza.

And what of the demands that Hamas had fought for and Gazans died for? The main demand, which was not just Hamas's, was for the lifting of the illegal seven-year Israeli blockade of Gaza, the reopening of the borders and the release of prisoners. Other specific demands included the rebuilding of Gaza international airport, the reopening of the 'safe passage' to the West Bank and the building of a sea port. The first three demands were already part of earlier agreements that Israel had violated. As to the last three, they were already agreed upon in the 1993 Oslo Accords, which, at the time, Hamas had vehemently opposed.

Indeed, after the Accords were signed Hamas used every means at its disposal to defeat the agreement, which it claimed was a capitulation. Likewise Netanyahu, who was leader of the opposition party, mobilised against it and against the leader of the Labour Party, Yitzhak Rabin, who signed it. Rabin was killed by a right-wing religious zealot. What little hope for a peaceful settlement that Oslo had promised went up in smoke. Now both sides who stood against the Accords are engaged in a deadly fight, with Hamas calling for concessions that it had rejected earlier. Netanyahu won the leadership of his country and Hamas gained popularity and a stronger political role within the Palestinian political configuration. It is the people on both sides who have been deprived of a life of peace and security.

At the end of this latest aggression Netanyahu's popularity plummeted, yet there was no call for an early election. And the Right is still in ascendancy. Netanyahu announced the appropriation of 988 acres near Bethlehem in the West Bank to be used for building yet more Jewish settlements. By claiming the land as 'state land' he was using that same old legal trick that I and so many others had proved time and again is contrary to municipal and international law.[16]

In September 2014, while the last ceasefire was in place, delegations from Israel and the Palestinian Authority went to Cairo to negotiate through Egyptian mediators. As the negotiations proceeded, the reconciliation between Hamas and Fatah was strained. Complicated talks proceeded, trying to reconcile Israel's perceived worries and its refusal to end the siege. However one looks at our situation, it all comes down to the simple fact that as long as Israel rejects peace, everything about our tiny area of the world will continue to look complicated and insoluble.

One of the primary ways in which Israel holds on to its military occupation and control over Palestinian society is through intelligence gathering. Forty-three members of Unit 8200, the IDF intelligence unit, recently signed a letter addressed to the Israeli prime minister and others, asserting that the information gathered and stored in the army's systems 'harms innocent people. It is used for political persecution and to create divisions within Palestinian society by recruiting collaborators and driving parts of Palestinian society against itself.'[17] The same point was made by Gideon Levy, who explained that the aim of this unit 'involves not only intelligence gathering and espionage, but also mechanism to control, extort and exploit the Palestinian population under occupation by erecting an enormous army of collaborators and informers, recruited through the vicious exploitation of their weaknesses, needs, illnesses and sexual orientation'. In their Arabic studies, we are told, 'they were taught all the forms of the Arabic word for "homosexual" – because they need it. They were required to find out about the sexual orientation, health and financial problems of tens of thousands of individuals.'[18]

As long as peace remains elusive, Israel is bound to continue to gather intelligence that it will utilise to create divisions and mayhem in our society. But once Israel begins to pursue policies seeking a peaceful resolution to the conflict much will change. Seemingly insurmountable security problems will begin to seem much simpler and more straightforward to resolve.

No sophisticated surveillance equipment or repressive mass arrests and intimidation can ever give Israel protection. The Eretz crossing from Gaza into Israel employed the most sophisticated surveillance equipment to a ridiculous extent, humiliating tens of thousands of Gazans who had to cross to go to work, for medical treatment or simply to visit relatives in the West Bank. Israel thought this would make it safe. Human beings can tolerate humiliation for a certain time but not for ever. Gaza militants found a way to dig under the closely monitored border and cross into Israel. Israel's belief in the efficacy of sophisticated equipment to bring it security is exaggerated and misplaced.

When this latest war ended, it came as no surprise to find that Israel could not be beaten militarily. Any idea that the pain, suffering and loss of income caused to Israel would prompt a rethink proved to be groundless. Is there anything, then, that can give us, the people of the region, hope for the future?

8

SEARCHING FOR JUSTICE

Where should we go after the last frontiers,
Where should the birds fly after the last sky ...

Mahmoud Darwish, *The Earth is Closing on Us*

It used to make me feel hopeful whenever I heard that the moderates in our region were gaining strength. It had always seemed to me a positive development when the power of rejectionists and hardliners is weakened. This, I thought, would remove the impediments to peace. But when, on 1 September 2014, Benjamin Netanyahu placed himself and Israel among the forces of moderation, I found yet another term that had been vitiated and stripped of its true meaning.

The initial sustained resistance to occupation during the first Intifada was mainly non-violent, but it was suppressed with such brutality that the sons who saw their fathers humiliated grew to be more violent. And the trend has continued ever since, with greater and greater levels of violence being used as Israel tries out more and more advanced and sophisticated weaponry that leads to more victims and more violence. Neither my father nor Yeshayahu Leibowitz was being naive when they proposed that the occupation should end and a political solution be found immediately after 1967, knowing as they did that time was of the essence. They realised that matters would only get more complicated as the years passed. New forces would arise and become entrenched and have vested interests in preserving the status quo. This is why they warned against waiting.

Nearly fifty years later, the violence continues, but new voices outside the area are beginning to be heard. Archbishop Desmond Tutu has said, 'There is no military solution to the conflict in the Holy Land. Violence begets violence, which begets more hatred and violence. Nor have the world's political and diplomatic leaders succeeded over many years to engineer a just and sustainable peace. Civil society must step into the breach, as it did in South Africa's struggle against apartheid.'[1]

Civil society can lend its help by supporting the Boycott, Divestment and Sanctions Movement's campaign against Israel. The terrible suffering of the people of Gaza that was witnessed globally and on social media gave it a huge boost. As far afield as Oakland in the USA, in a show of solidarity for the people of Gaza port workers delayed the unloading of cargo from an Israeli Zim vessel for days after its arrival. The campaign was also effective on the home front in the

West Bank, which constitutes a major market for Israeli goods. Previously, while the Palestinians were calling on the world to boycott Israel, back home the boycott of Israeli products was not successful. It was the war in Gaza that gave the extra impetus for that particular struggle. And the reason for that is because the struggle there proved that it is possible to win. Prior to this people were too defeated to even try challenging Israel. Placards in Ramallah called on people not to buy Israeli products, saying 'Don't pay for the bullets that kill Palestinian youth' and showing photographs of the innocent young face of Mohammed Abu Khdeir and others.

A more correct term for the BDS Movement's campaign is, I believe, a counter-boycott. We Palestinians in the occupied territories have been suffering from Israel's boycott throughout the forty-seven years of occupation. This takes many forms, including restriction on movement and limitations on civil liberties, in addition to a number of specific prohibitions that complicate our lives and limit our freedom, such as the restriction on imports of Arabic books from Arab countries that have not made peace with Israel. Lebanon, which is the main producer of Arabic books, falls into this category. Except for those Palestinians living in Jerusalem, the city as well as the rest of Israel is forbidden to us. Tens of thousands of Palestinians have been denied residency in Jerusalem and the West Bank and Gaza and are not even allowed in to visit. This is why we consider the boycott against Israel a counter-boycott.

Our hope must lie with people, not governments. Anyone with an iota of political sense would realise that governments are always the last to act. It has to be people who keep up the pressure and use their immense collective power, just as happened in the struggle to end the apartheid regime in South Africa.

Boycott is often harsh and indiscriminate, yet it is necessary. Palestinians inside Israel, who constitute 20 per cent of the population, might suffer if, out of the taxes they pay to the state, they manage to get subsidies for their cultural work. If Salim Dao and his singer daughter, Maysa, say, were to receive Israeli state funding and they wished to perform in Europe, the boycott would apply to them.

Nadine Gordimer, the South African writer who struggled for most of her life against apartheid, once told me that when she visited New York during the apartheid era she went into a shop on Fifth Avenue to buy some gadget her son wanted. She found what she needed and was about to pay when the shop assistant asked her where she came from. When she told him South Africa, he said, 'I'm sorry, madam, I cannot sell you this.' She had a bittersweet smile as she told me the story.

In a recent article Zeev Sternhell wrote: 'The West's political elite is not speaking out openly against Israeli colonialism, for fear of encouraging the anti-Semitic monster. But at the universities and in the schools, in the media and on social networks, they are already saying this explicitly: It is untenable that the Jewish past serve as a justification for cruelty in the Palestinian present.'[2]

Many who are against the boycott claim that it is anti-Semitic to call for the boycott of Israel. But is it? Is being anti-Israel the same as being anti-Semitic? When does anti-Israel become anti-Jew?

The struggle of the people of Palestine for self-determination has become one of the greatest issues of our time. As such, and like many a popular international struggle, it attracts all sorts of people, not least anti-Semites. To most people involved in the struggle for Palestinian rights, the distinction is clear. Not every Jew is a Zionist and not every Zionist is actively involved in supporting Israel or is uncritical of its treatment of Palestinians. Over the years, large numbers of Jews from all parts of the world have been actively involved in the struggle for Palestinian rights. Israel does its best to conflate the two and claim all Jews for its cause, much to the distress of many Jews around the world who want to be left alone and should have the right to stay away from the entire conflict and not be implicated, if they so choose.

This is not to deny that many Jews around the world who do not necessarily see themselves as Zionists still feel a certain affinity with Israel. This is their choice and they should not be held accountable for Israel's behaviour. However, to the extent that they support Israel by money or in other ways, they cannot escape taking responsibility for its violations of the rights of Palestinians; the same holds true for American evangelists who support settlements in the West Bank. Anti-Semitism has a long history and is a vicious type of racism, but that does not mean that Jews who actively support Israel with money or otherwise are not complicit in Israel's racist policies.

What should also be recognised is the way Jews in Europe and the US, after the rise in secularism in these societies, have been raised to understand the meaning of being Jewish in terms of the Holocaust and its relationship to Israel, seeing the country as a response to the worst manifestation of anti-Semitism. So when those who suffer the excesses of Israel criticise its actions, many Jews feel this is an attack on their Jewish identity and therefore call these attacks anti-Semitic.

I believe that it is part of Israel's psychological war against the Palestinians to portray the country as standing not alone but with the active support of Jewish communities all over the world. The implication then is that it's unrealistic for the Palestinians to believe that they can defeat Israel and its mission of settling all the land of Greater Israel with Jews. Rather, Palestinians should submit to the Israeli view that the occupied territories do not belong to them but to Jews all over the world.

The resolution of these fundamental issues is necessary for the position of Israel to be normalised, enabling it to be accepted in the region. But if there is to be peace in our region the Palestinians also need to come to terms with the existence of Israel and accept that its people are here to stay. What we should seek is not the destruction of Israeli society, but ways to forge a new relationship that would make it possible for both of us to have a full life based on justice and equality in this beautiful but tortured land which we share, for both of us – Palestinian Arabs and Israeli Jews – live here.

The Gaza war was the first time that Palestinians stood their ground, despite the massive assault, and succeeded in inflicting harm on Israel by fighting back. Jenin's resistance during the 2002 Israeli invasion of the West Bank was another example, but on a much smaller and more limited scale. After the attack on Gaza Defence Minister

Moshe Ya'alon said, 'The fact that a 20,000 strong terror group has endured for 50 days against the strongest army in the Middle East and has stayed in power – it bothers me very much.'[3]

How the success of this Islamic group will affect Palestinian young people is yet to be seen. Will it perhaps mark the beginning of a belief that militarisation is the only way to force Israel's hand? Much will depend on Israel.

As the war was still raging, Hamas and the people of Gaza said they were tired of conflict and were exhausted, but they did not want to stop before the ordeal of their siege ended. The pain of this latest round of aggression will remain with us for many years. Those who lost loved ones or were maimed in the fighting might never forget. Their only solace would be if their suffering was not in vain, because it ushered a period of peace.

The future is for the youth on both sides. On the Palestinian side, the coming generation will have so many memories of shameful defeats and instances of discrimination and humiliation. They will perhaps draw strength from the brave resistance that Palestinian fighters put up in Gaza in the summer of 2014. If Israel refuses to withdraw from the territories occupied in 1967 and negotiate with the Palestinians about all outstanding issues and rights, the Palestinians will have to choose between life without land and rights, or life with dignity. If this is the choice and the other side refuses to let go, they will eventually do what it takes, fighting to the bitter end. The Israelis also have the choice of either remaining eternally mobilised for war or coming to terms with the existence of the Palestinians and recognising their right to self-determination.

Children and poets should be trusted more than politicians. They are better at imagining a better future. An eleven-year-old Israeli girl called Ohad, who spent most of her summer holiday in 2014 in bomb shelters in Sderot, in the south of Israel, drew a simple comic with five panels. In the first a plane bearing the colours of the Palestinian flag is flying in the sky. In the second a plane bearing the colours of the Israeli flag is flying in the sky. In the third the two planes have a head-on collision. In the fourth the explosion results in many hearts that fall to the ground. In the last drawing the multicoloured hearts are collected by Palestinians on one side of the border and Israelis on the other.

In conclusion, here is a piece by the Irish poet Seamus Heaney, written before his country, Northern Ireland, managed to find reconciliation:

Human beings suffer,
They torture one another,
They get hurt and get hard.
No poem or play or song
Can fully right a wrong
Inflicted and endured.

The innocent in gaols
Beat on their bars together.
A hunger-striker's father
Stands in the graveyard dumb.
The police widow in veils
Faints at the funeral home.

History says, don't hope
On this side of the grave.
But then, once in a lifetime
The longed-for tidal wave
Of justice can rise up,
And hope and history rhyme.

So hope for a great sea-change
On the far side of revenge.
Believe that further shore
Is reachable from here.
Believe in miracle
And cures and healing wells.

Call miracle self-healing:
The utter, self-revealing
Double-take of feeling.
If there's fire on the mountain
Or lightning and storm
And a god speaks from the sky

That means someone is hearing
The outcry and the birth-cry
Of new life at its term.[4]

GLOSSARY

ahlan	Arabic: hello, welcome
akub	Arabic: gundelia (*Gundelia tournefortii*)
aliya	Hebrew: ascent
Al-Watan	Arabic: lit. the homeland. This was the name used by a settler company to register Palestinian land.
Eretz Israel	Hebrew: the Land of Israel
fedayeen	Arabic: freedom fighters
irhab	Arabic: terrorism
irhabiyeen	Arabic: terrorists
ma'abar	Hebrew: crossing; pl. *ma'abarot*
mahboub el Arab	Arabic: beloved by the Arabs
makhsheer	Hebrew: walkie-talkie
makhsom	Hebrew: checkpoint

mukhareb	Arabic: destroyer; pl. *mukharebeen*. Used by the Israelis to mean 'vandal', as in '*Anta mukhareb*' ('You are a vandal').
must'arab'een	Arabic: Arabist. Used in the occupied territories to refer to Israelis pretending to be Arabs coming to make arrests.
mutasalilun	Arabic: infiltrators
Nakba	Arabic: lit. catastrophe. The Palestinian term for the events of 1948, when more than 700,000 Palestinians fled or were expelled from their homes and Palestine vanished from the map, to be replaced by the State of Israel.
natsh	Arabic: poterium thorn (*Poterium spinosum*)
ramzor	Hebrew: traffic lights (pronounced *ramzon* in Arabic)
shabab	Arabic: youth
shababnikkim	Hebrew (slang): right-wing ultra-Orthodox extremist youths
sumoud	Arabic: steadfastness, endurance, perseverance
umbaz	Arabic (colloquial): traditional dress
walla	Arabic: 'by Allah'
yom yom	Hebrew: daily
Zochrot	Hebrew: lit. remembering. This organisation undertakes projects to promote understanding of the Nakba and the Palestinian right to return.

NOTES

1. 1948: Infiltrating Back Home

1. In June 2014 Mordehai Amihai of Israel was appointed vice-chair to represent the Western European and Other Groups voting bloc on the Special Committee on Decolonisation at the 69th session of the UN General Assembly. Part of the committee's role was to consider matters relating to Palestine and Palestinian refugees. Arab countries tried and failed to thwart his appointment.

2. The full definition of an absentee, according to the Israel Absentee Property Law of 1950, is 'a person who, at any time during the period between 29 November 1947 and the day on which a declaration is published under section 9(d) of the Law and Administration Ordinance of 1948 that the state of emergency declared by the Provision Council of State on 19 May 1948 has

134

ceased to exist, was a legal owner of any property situated in the area of Israel ... and who at any time during the said period (i) was a national or citizen of the Lebanon, Egypt, Syria, Saudi Arabia, Trans-Jordan, Iraq or the Yemen, or (ii) was in one of these countries or in any part of Palestine outside the area of Israel, or (iii) was a Palestinian citizen and left his ordinary place of residence in Palestine (a) for a place outside Palestine before 1 September 1948; or (b) for a place held at the time by forces which sought to prevent the establishment of the State of Israel or which fought against it after its establishment ...'

3. The Palestinian Authority was established in 1995 to take over some responsibilities from the Israeli military government with regard to governing the Palestinian population in the West Bank and Gaza Strip.

4. Josh Chester, 'Blurred lines: Palestinians to ask UN to swap Green Line for red one', *Haaretz*, 16 March 2014.

5. Edward Said, 'The one-state solution', *New York Times Magazine*, 10 January 1999.

6. Alona Ferber, 'Three interviews with Israel's smallest minority', *Haaretz*, 20 June 2014. According to Ferber, 92 per cent of Israel's 50,000 asylum seekers are from Sudan and Eritrea. Most came to Israel after 2007. The Israeli government is also promoting the 'voluntary departure' of African asylum seekers, 4,000 of whom have left the country since December 2013.

7. Azoulay's essay was published as part of the series 'Apparatus, Capture, Trace' in a supplement to *Fillip* 16, edited by Kate Steinmann.

8. Gideon Levy and Alex Levac, 'Drafting the blueprint for Palestinian refugees' right of return', *Haaretz*, 5 October 2013.
9. From the collection *Never Mind: Twenty Poems and a Story*, translated by Peter Cole, Yahya Hijazi and Gabriel Levin (Ibis Editions, 2000), pp. 58–9.
10. The quote from Moshe Dayan and the information about the transfer committee are from Arik Ariel, 'Revealed from the archive: Israel's secret plan to resettle Arab refugees', *Haaretz*, 19 December 2013.
11. Amira Hass, 'Poll: Nearly a third of Gazans have relatives in WB, E. J'lm or Israel', *Haaretz*, 18 December 2013. According to Hass, 'The difficulty is seen in the surveyed subjects' answer to a question regarding the maintenance of ties with relatives in other parts of the country. About 70 percent maintain such ties, but only 13 percent out of those who do maintain ties meet their relatives face to face inside the country's borders. About 81 percent of those who keep in touch with their relatives living a few dozen kilometers away are only able to do so by telephone, internet or mail. Another roughly 6 percent meet their relatives abroad.'
12. See http://www.al-monitor.com/pulse/originals/2013/06/naftali-bennett-blunt-speech.html#ixzz2j0gdvQte.
13. A letter from the British Foreign Secretary Arthur James Balfour addressed to Lord Rothschild, stating: 'His Majesty's Government view with favour the establishment in Palestine of a national home for the Jewish people, and will use their best endeavours to facilitate the achievement of this object, it being clearly understood that nothing shall be done which

may prejudice the civil and religious rights of existing non-Jewish communities in Palestine, or the rights and political status enjoyed by Jews in any other country.'

2. 1967: Settling the Occupied Territories

1. Gideon Levy and Alex Levac, '"It was nothing personal," bereaved Palestinian father told', *Haaretz*, 4 April 2014.
2. Gil Hilel, 'Breaking the silence: In the reality of occupation, there are no Palestinian civilians – only potential terrorists', *Independent*, 16 June 2013.
3. Simon Jenkins, 'The last thing Norway needs is illiberal Britain's patronising', *Guardian*, 26 July 2011.

3. 1993: Oslo Accords – a Post-Mortem

1. The peace conference was hosted by Spain and co-sponsored by the United States and the Soviet Union to start the Israeli–Palestinian peace process through negotiations involving Israel, the Palestinians and Arab countries, including Jordan, Lebanon and Syria.
2. I discuss this subject at greater length in 'The Weight of Legal History: Constraints and Hopes in the Search for a Sovereign Legal Language', in *The Arab–Israeli Accords: Legal Perspectives*, edited by Eugene Cotran and Chibli Mallat (CIMEL, SOAS and Kluwer Law International, 1996).

3. Aziz Shehadeh, Fuad Shehadeh and Raja Shehadeh, 'Israeli Proposed Road Plan for the West Bank: A Question for the International Court of Justice' (Al-Haq, 1984).

4. For a full review of the question whether or not it was right to boycott elections (where the author reaches a different conclusion), see Michael Dumper, *Jerusalem Unbound: Geography, History and the Future of the Holy City* (Columbia University Press, 2014), pp. 67–74.

5. Ari Shavit, *My Promised Land* (Random House, 2013), p. 221. The mention of 'Labor' refers to the Labour Party, which was the main ruling party for many years after the establishment of the State of Israel.

6. Raja Shehadeh, *From Occupation to Interim Accords: Israel and the Palestinian Territories*, with forewords by Ian Brownlie and Edward Said (CIMEL, SOAS and Kluwer Law International, 1997).

7. Chaim Levinson, 'IDF seized West Bank house despite court ruling for Palestinian owners', *Haaretz*, 9 December 2013.

4. 2003: The Wall

1. Yeshayahu Leibowitz, 'The Territories', 1968, in *Judaism, Jewish Values, and the Jewish State*, edited and translated by Eliezer Goldman (Harvard University Press, 1995), pp. 225–6.

2. Avi Raz, *The Bride and the Dowry: Israel, Jordan, and the Palestinians in the Aftermath of the June 1967 War* (Yale

University Press, 2012). See especially pp. 7–8 and pp. 27–8.

3. Amira Hass, 'And in other Holocaust-related news ...', *Haaretz*, 28 January 2014.

4. Edward Said, 'Memory, Inequality and Power: Palestine and the Universality of Human Rights', lecture given on 29 January 2003. See http://www.thefreelibrary.com/ Memory,+inequality,+and+power %3A+Palestine+and+the+universality+of...-a0126387261

5. For a full discussion of the annexation and its limits, see Michael Dumper, *Jerusalem Unbound: Geography, History and the Future of the Holy City* (Columbia University Press, 2014), pp. 60–66.

6. On 1 November 1981 the Military Commander of the Israeli forces in the West Bank declared the creation of a Civilian Administration by Military Order No. 947. Section 2 of the order lists 162 military orders which the Head of the Civilian Administration is charged with administering. On 23 November 1995, after the Oslo Accords were signed, Military Proclamation No. 7 was issued by the Israeli military in the West Bank. Article 4 of the Proclamation declares that 'the Commander of the Israeli army in the area and the Head of the Civilian Administration shall transfer to the [Palestinian] Council and its agencies, powers and responsibilities exercised by them or other delegates including legislative, judicial and executive powers' as specified in the Interim Agreement [of 1995]. For a full study of the Civilian Administration, see Raja Shehadeh and Jonathan Kuttab, 'Civilian Administration in the Occupied West Bank:

Analysis of Israeli Military Government Order No. 947',
January 1982, Al-Haq publication online.

7. Fredrik Dahl and Lennart Simonsson, 'Israel has 80 of
the world's 16,300 nuclear warheads', *Haaretz*, 17 June
2014.

8. Barak Ravid, 'UN nuclear assembly rejects Arab bid
criticizing Israel's "atomic arsenal"', *Haaretz*, 25
September 2014.

9. Yossi Klein, 'Look! An Arab speaking Hebrew', *Haaretz*,
12 July 2013. Originally established in 1952, Unit 8200
is an Israeli intelligence corps responsible for collecting
signals intelligence and code decryption. For more on
Unit 8200, see Chapter 7.

10. *To the East: Orientalism in the Arts in Israel*, exh. cat., Israel
Museum, Jerusalem, Summer 1998, p. vi.

11. 'Last night, 11 January 2012, at 9 pm, the Israeli Supreme
Court in a 6–5 decision, delivered a 232-page judgment
upholding the constitutionality of the Citizenship
and Entry into Israel Law – 2003 (as amended 2007).
This law severely restricts Palestinian Arab citizens
of Israel from living together in Israel with their
Palestinian spouses from the Occupied Palestinian
Territory (OPT) or from "enemy states" defined by the
law as "Syria, Lebanon, Iran and Iraq". Thousands of
Palestinian families are affected by this law, forced to
move abroad, or live apart or to live together illegally
in Israel.' See http://adalah.org/eng/Articles/1185/
Israeli-Supreme-Court-Upholds-Ban-on-Family.

5. 2013: The Beginning of the End of Negotiations

1. On 2 December 2013, the fully armed and trained Ninth
   Palestinian Battalion entered Nablus 'to safeguard the
   inhabitants in the entire district and establish law and
   order there'. When interviewed, the Palestinian head of
   the battalion, Muhammad Hammoudeh, was at pains to
   justify this deployment as beneficial to the inhabitants
   of the district, claiming the aim was to provide
   protection from lawless elements and to safeguard
   the security of the Palestinian population there. But
   everyone knew about the failure of an earlier similar
   operation in Jenin. There many of the lawbreakers
   managed to escape to Area C, under full Israeli security
   control, where Palestinian law enforcers cannot pursue
   them. The larger tragedy was that many of the residents
   of the Nablus district were suffering repeatedly from
   attacks to their lands and person from Jewish settlers
   living in nearby settlements. A few weeks earlier, on 13
   November, a Palestinian home was set on fire by settlers
   in the village of Sinjil, south of Nablus. Following the
   arson attack the Israeli military said that it considers
   incidents of this kind serious and that they undermine
   security in the region. But their words were not followed
   by any effective action against the perpetrators. Against
   such attacks the fully equipped Ninth Battalion can
   do nothing. And yet Hammoudeh was speaking of
   providing 'security' for the Palestinians and planning to
   collect all illegal weapons because, he said, 'We are one
   authority. The only arms must be those of the national
   authority held by the security forces.' All this means that

farmers in the Nablus region, whose land and homes are
threatened by the aggressive settlers living nearby, are
left to fend for themselves. Recently some of them have
been setting metal traps that were used in the past to
protect the land from deer and wild boar.

2. 'It has been said that Israel always sells a "concession"
three times: once when promising it, once when signing
an official agreement about it and thirdly when actually
fulfilling the undertaking. This happened when the time
came to implement the third withdrawal from the West
Bank under the Oslo agreements, which never happened'
(Uri Avnery, 'Why the Palestinian–Israeli talks bubble
burst', *Redress, Information & Analysis*, 11 April 2014).

3. Danny Gutwein, 'Some comments on the class
foundations of the occupation', *MRZine Monthly*, 6
June 2006. In further more recent confirmation of this
process, the renowned Israeli journalist Amira Hass has
written: 'As the past 30 years have shown, settlements
flourish as the welfare state contracts. They offer
ordinary people what their salaries would not allow
them in sovereign Israel, within the borders of June
4, 1967: cheap land, large homes, benefits, subsidies,
wide-open spaces, a view, a superior road network and
quality education. Even for those Israeli Jews who have
not moved there, the settlements illuminate their
horizon as an option for a social and economic upgrade.
That option is more real than the vague promise of
peacetime improvements, an unknown situation ...
People who have gotten used to privilege under a system
based on ethnic discrimination see its abrogation as a

threat to their welfare' ('Israel knows that peace just doesn't pay', *Haaretz*, 11 May 2009).

4. At the time of the negotiations there were numerous reports in the Israeli press that senior European diplomats were meeting with their Israeli counterparts and letting them know that there would be continued European sanctions against the settlements. '"The marking of produce from the [Palestinian] territories is on hold at this stage," [a senior] European diplomat said to his Israeli interlocutor. "However, should the negotiations with the Palestinians run aground you should expect a deluge of sanctions." The Israeli official was taken aback by the sharp words. "Aren't the circumstances of a breakdown in negotiations relevant?" he asked. The European replied laconically, "The way things look now, you will be the losers in the blame game"' (Barak Ravid, 'Swell of boycotts driving Israel into international isolation', *Haaretz*, 12 December 2013).

5. Chemi Shalev, '"Pro-Israel" discussion in New York ends in walkout, insults and recriminations', *Haaretz*, 17 December 2013.

6. Barak Ravid, 'EU set to offer massive aid to Israel, Palestinians for peace deal', *Haaretz*, 13 December 2013. According to Ravid, 'A senior European diplomat, who asked to remain anonymous because of the sensitivity of the matter, said a draft of the policy decision was approved yesterday at a meeting of the EU's Political and Security Committee in Brussels. Ambassadors to the EU from the organisation's 28 member states attended the meeting. The draft resolution, a copy of which was obtained by *Haaretz*, details the economic, political and

military aid the EU hopes will encourage Israel and the
Palestinians to agree to the painful compromises that a
peace agreement will inevitably entail.'

7. *Maariv*, 14 April 2013.
8. Dvora Morag's mother was speaking on a video prepared
    for Morag's exhibition *And You Shall Tell Your Daughter*,
    curated by Ktsia Alon at Zochrot's Visual Research
    Laboratory, 12 December 2013–30 January 2014. As the
    Zochrot website makes clear, 'War, becoming a refugee,
    fleeing to save your life, the fear of death gnawing at
    you mercilessly – these are basic human experiences,
    independent of time and place.'
9. Zeev Sternhell, 'Unconditional Palestinian surrender',
    Haaretz, 18 April 2014.
10. The Israeli Military Commander in the West Bank began
    using the ploy of appropriating land for the exclusive
    use of Jewish settlers on the ground that it is 'state land'
    after the decision in 1979 of the Israeli High Court of
    Justice in the Elon Moreh case, when the court rejected
    the order by the military to requisition Palestinian land
    near the Palestinian city of Nablus for the use of the
    settlers. After this decision the Israeli military completed
    its survey of Palestinian land and proceeded (contrary
    to international law) to declare any unregistered land
    as state land. With very few exceptions most of the
    land declared by the Israeli military as state land does
    not fall under this category according to the local law
    and should not be reserved for the exclusive use of the
    occupier under international law. For a fuller discussion
    of the Elon Moreh case, see Raja Shehadeh, *Occupier's Law:*

Israel and the West Bank (Institute for Palestine Studies, Washington, DC, 1985), pp. 18–22.

11. Henry Siegman, 'Why America is irrelevant to Middle East peacemaking', *Haaretz*, 8 April 2014.
12. Peter Beinart, 'Obama should make Israelis look at themselves in the mirror', *Haaretz*, 9 April 2014.
13. Middle East Peace Talks: Q&A, Peter Beaumont, *Guardian*, 29 April 2014.
14. Ora Cohan and Rotem Starkman, 'Naftali Bennett: No need to give peace a chance', *Haaretz*, 19 May 2014.

6. Spring 2014

1. See http://www.youtube.com/watch?v=a1s3Qt-Tm5I.
2. Not only did the strike fail to end the practice of administrative detention but in June 2014 the Security Cabinet decided to make the conditions of Palestinian security prisoners stricter. However, it seemed to be finding it difficult to think of ways to make this happen. Permission to pursue academic studies and complete matriculation exams had already been cancelled and the number of television channels the prisoners were allowed to watch was reduced, while those they were allowed to watch did not include Arabic news channels.
3. Editorial, 'Simply because he was bored', *Haaretz*, 30 May 2014.
4. Quoted in Mark Landler, 'Melancholy after a failed peace effort', *International New York Times*, 7 July 2014.

5. 'Both Abbas and chief negotiator Erekat say rightly that the Americans never gave them a copy of the framework document, but only presented ideas orally. They could thus not peruse the paper thoroughly and formulate an opinion. At this time, drafts of the document were being exchanged between Washington and Jerusalem on a daily basis. The Palestinians' response, when they grasped what was going on, was that they were being duped. So great was their suspiciousness and so intense their frustration with the Americans that they lost interest in the process completely.

    '"The Americans did not invest enough time in the Palestinians," a senior Israeli official related. "They didn't hold video talks with them or discussions into the night over every letter in the document. The result was a crisis of expectations. How many times did we say to them: What about Mahmoud Abbas? Did you talk to him? Does he agree to all these points? The Americans neglected Mahmoud Abbas throughout this period, and when Kerry came to him in Paris it was already too late"' (Barak Ravid, 'The secret fruits of the peace talks, a future point of departure?', *Haaretz*, 5 July 2014).

6. Chemi Shalev, 'Netanyahu's new Middle East equations: Iraq=Iran and Hamas=Al-Qaida + ISIS', *Haaretz*, 23 June 2014.

7. Gilad Shalit, an Israeli soldier, was captured on 25 June 2006 and continued to be held by Hamas for 1,934 days until a prisoners' exchange agreement was signed in Egypt for the release of 1,027 mainly Palestinian prisoners.

8. Jonathan Lis, 'Kidnapped teens' mothers slam PM for deal that ended prison hunger strike', *Haaretz*, 25 June 2014.

9. Editorial, 'What is the aim of Israel's show of force', *Haaretz*, 23 June 2014.

10. Ibid.

11. Quoted in Steven Erlanger, 'Extremism leads Israelis to look within', *International Herald Tribune*, 11 July 2014.

12. Yehudit Karp, *Karp Report: Israeli Investigation into Settler Violence Against Palestinians on the West Bank* (Institute for Palestine Studies, Washington, DC, 1985).

13. Raja Shehadeh, *New Yorker*, 9 July 2014.

14. Chemi Shalev, 'Berlin, 1933 and Jerusalem, 2014: when racist thugs are on the prowl', *Haaretz*, 3 July 2014.

15. Chris Hedges, 'Israel is captive to its "destructive process"', Truthdig, 14 July 2014.

7. War on Gaza

1. Nir Hasson, '"Kids' Intifada": jails fill with juvenile rioters', *Haaretz*, 19 September 2014. As Hasson reports, hundreds of juveniles were arrested.

2. Linda Butler, 'Suicide bombers: dignity, despair, and the need for hope. An interview with Eyad El Sarraj', *Journal of Palestine Studies*, Vol. 31, No. 4 (Summer 2002), pp. 71–6.

3. Amira Hass, 'Reaping what we have sown in Gaza', *Haaretz*, 21 July 2014.

4. Harriet Sherwood, 'Palestinians returning home find Israeli troops left faeces and venomous graffiti', *Guardian*, 7 August 2014.

5. Statement from explosives engineering police of the Gaza Ministry of Interior, reported in Ma'an News Agency on 17 September 2014. Among the deadly weapons fired on the Gaza Strip were flechette shells, fuel-air bombs (which explode twice, including after impact) and dime shells. Some 8,000 explosives were fired from war planes alone, many more from land and sea.

6. Idan Barir, +972 Blog, 8 August 2014.

7. Adam Taylor, 'Israel hopes phone calls to Palestinians will save lives. It ends up looking Orwellian', *Washington Post*, 17 July 2014.

8. Steven Poole, 'On Gaza and the misleading language of war', *Guardian*, 9 August 2014.

9. Uri Avnery, 'Israel's ever-changing goals, and its tunnel vision', *Redress Information & Analysis*, 2 August 2014.

10. Quoted in Zeev Sternhell, 'In midst of Gaza strife, now's the time for Israel to seek a treaty with the Palestinians', *Haaretz*, 18 July 2014.

11. Benny Morris, 'We must defeat Hamas – next time', *Haaretz*, 30 July 2014. The article continues: 'This will require months of combat, during which the Strip will be cleansed, neighborhood by neighborhood, of Hamas and Islamic Jihad operatives and armaments. It will exact a serious price in lives from both Israel Defense Forces soldiers and Palestinian civilians. But that's the price required of a nation like ours, which wants to live on its own land in a neighborhood like ours. After

gaining control of Gaza, it must be hoped that some moderate Arab power, perhaps the Palestinian Authority, will take over the reins of government.'

12. 'Peres: Gaza rockets make future West Bank pullout harder to justify', *Haaretz*, 13 August 2014.

13. Gideon Levy, 'Nothing will come of Israel's quiet', *Haaretz*, 17 August 2014.

14. Raja Shehadeh, *The Sealed Room* (Quartet, 1992), p. 181.

15. From the UN Office for the Coordination of Humanitarian Affairs, Occupied Palestinian Territories (OACHA).

16. Raja Shehadeh, 'The land law of Palestine: An analysis of the definition of state lands', *Journal of Palestine Studies*, Vol. 11, No. 2 (Winter 1982), pp. 82–99.

17. Gili Cohen, 'Reservists from elite IDF intel unit refuse to serve over Palestinian "persecution"', *Haaretz*, 12 September 2014.

18. Gideon Levy, 'Revolt in the Stasi', *Haaretz*, 14 September 2014.

8. Searching for Justice

1. Archbishop Desmond Tutu, in a message of support to the Russell Tribunal, 20 August 2014.

2. Zeev Sternhell, 'It's the colonialism they hate, not Jews', *Haaretz*, 19 September 2014.

3. 'Ya'alon touts Israeli victory in Gaza; Lieberman's not so sure', *Haaretz*, 29 August 2014.

4. Seamus Heaney, *The Cure at Troy* (Faber and Faber, 1990).

ACKNOWLEDGEMENTS

I wish to express my gratitude to the members of the Edward Said Memorial Lecture Executive Committee for their invitation to give the 2013 lecture, on which this book is based. It was what started me thinking about the themes explored here.

The first draft was much improved by the advice and editorial skills of Alex Baramki. My thanks to him.

In the spring of 2014, when the US-sponsored negotiations between Palestine and Israel collapsed, I was ready to send my manuscript for publication. But then many important developments took place that had to be included. It was difficult and painful to follow the unfolding sad and wrenching developments of that spring and the even more heartbreaking summer when the war on Gaza was raging. I would not have been able to write about this time without the support of family and friends, who endured more of my long, silent reveries than usual.

Once completed, the manuscript was reviewed by my editor and publisher, Andrew Franklin, and Penny Daniel. I am grateful to both for their contributions, as I am to the rest of the team at Profile, especially to my publicist, Valentina Zanca.

Lesley Levene went through the manuscript doing more than a copy editor usually does, providing comments and seeking clarification where needed, checking endnotes and making stylistic suggestions that improved the flow. My sincere thanks to Lesley.